Symbolic Mythology

Symbolic Mythology

Interpretations of the Myths of Ancient Greece and Rome

John Fiore

Writers Club Press

San Jose New York Lincoln Shanghai

Symbolic Mythology
Interpretations of the Myths of Ancient Greece and Rome

All Rights Reserved © 2001 by John Fiore

Writers Club Press
an imprint of iUniverse, Inc.

For information address:
iUniverse, Inc.
5220 S. 16th St., Suite 200
Lincoln, NE 68512
www.iuniverse.com

ISBN: 0-595-20400-7

Printed in the United States of America

To Debs - my wife, my muse, and an all-around fabulous chick.

CONTENTS

Part 1

Power and Purpose

THE RAGE OF TYPHOS

"Let the fires of retribution be quenched with the blood of Olympus!" roared the hundredth snake head of Typhos, spawn of Tartarus and Earth. "I am the bringer of doom to the children of the Titans! I am vengeance!"

The unthinkable had come to pass. Mother Earth, no longer able to remain a passive observer to the warring between her offspring and their children, had joined in horrific union with the hell-pit Tartarus, that abysmal chasm of eternal torment. From that union, she had birthed the monstrosity whose massive frame now shadowed the haven of Mount Olympus. The animals of the countryside fled the beast's path, for Typhos was a thing most appalling to behold; perverse in its shape and monolithic in its size, Typhos had risen from earth as a horror full-grown and immortal, and the gods themselves, though hidden in their palace, surely trembled at the sight of it.

"You will all burn!" the hundredth snake head cried out. "You will all scream for mercy, and still you shall burn! And what is not charred to ash and scattered across our mother, I shall devour!" The hundredth head cackled and hissed with delight as the other ninety-nine heads turned toward the palace of the gods atop Olympus. Each head, which spoke in a different animal voice, suddenly became quiet, and the maddening cacophony that had filled the sky ceased. Typhos stilled, its broad chest heaving in deeply. The eyes of every snake head then began to glow a fierce yellow beneath the slick black scales of its brows. The monster's mountain-sized hands balled into fists. The hundred snake heads shook violently as the glowing of the eyes blindingly intensified. "Die, now,

Olympus," screamed the hundredth head, its sickening black tongue flailing, "and let the Titans be avenged!"

Flames burst forth from every eye socket of the behemoth, and the powerful inferno engulfed miles of earth, sky, and sea. At the center of the conflagration was Mount Olympus itself, the mighty home of Zeus the Great Bearer of Lightning and his kin, the very seat of their power. Gone was it now from the sight of any living creature in the vicinity, for the deadly issuance of Typhos the avenger covered and scorched all.

When the monster's flaming wrath had expired, its multitude of eyes eagerly began searching for what remained of its prey. To the beast's surprise, the palace on Olympus had been severely burned, yet still it stood, likely due to its magical construction. More surprising than that, Typhos could find no bodies of gods. Surely, there should have been some remains left behind for him to enjoy. After all, they were gods. They could have withstood the onslaught to some degree. So, where were Hestia, Demeter, Hera, Hades, Poseidon, and, especially, Zeus? None had left the palace, but now, none were to be found. Several of the snake heads began to nervously mutter in a variety of guttural, animal sounds.

"Psst. Typhos." A low voice beckoned from the distance.

Half of the hundred heads swung around wildly looking for the source of the summons. The slimy, black serpent skulls surveyed the countryside, black tongues flicking away madly, but could find nothing, no god nor man who might call the Tartarus-spawn by name.

But there was a bull.

Most of the hundred heads continued to look around for the caller while the head of Typhos which spoke the language of bulls slinked downward to question the solitary animal as to its knowledge of the one who had spoken the monster's name. Perhaps it had seen something Typhos had not.

"Moo?" asked Typhos.

The bull replied, "Fool."

A bolt of lightning instantly pierced the throat of the bull-speaking head of the monster, sending a shower of sparks, black blood, and venom spattering across the base of Mount Olympus. The head squealed in pain as the rest of Typhos quaked in the unexpected agony. Before the monster had even realized what was happening, ten more of its heads were destroyed in similar fashion, most exploding into stumps of black slime from the force of the awesome bolts of the Great Thunderer.

"Zeus!" screamed the hundredth head, eyes already beginning to glow again.

"I do stand before you, fiend," responded the mighty King of Olympus, no longer in the guise of a bull, "and you find me ever ready to defend what is mine. My brethren were those whom you so thoughtlessly ignored as you stormed Olympus, disguised as the animals that fled without your notice. They shall support me in your destruction, should the need arise." The air crackled around Zeus's fists. "Come, Typhos! Test my wrath!"

Before the creature could react, another shaft of sharp, searing lightning lanced into its monstrousness, severing three heads at once and blinding a fourth. Typhos bellowed from the horrible wounding. Twenty other unscathed heads directed the creature's single gigantic body toward a nearby mountain. With little effort, Typhos ripped the mountain from the earth and flung it at mighty Zeus. The Bearer of Lightning was nimble enough to avoid the crushing blow, and, in full battle lust, quickly launched two more deadly lightning bolts into the mouths of his attacker.

Thus raged the battle, and all was shaken. The seas boiled, the land was seared, and even the Underworld quaked as the immortals warred with a ferocity that rivaled even that of the earlier battle between the Titans and the Olympians. Typhos tore up continents to use as missiles and spewed flames from his eyes, while Zeus fired off his endless supply of thunderbolts, with very few ever missing their marks.

At the end of the tumult, Zeus remained standing while Typhos lay sprawled across the land with all of his still-attached heads bearing the scorch marks of the lightning-wrath of the Lord of Olympus. As Typhos was immortal, he would always live on in some way, and Zeus knew that the threat of his return had best be diminished. The monster was too dangerous to consign to the prison of Tartarus, where the other Titans might restore him to his powerful self. Therefore, wise Zeus took up the very first mountain that Typhos had flung at him, Mount Aetna, and pounded it atop the creature's prone form. Almost immediately, the rock within the heart of the mountain began to melt from the heat of Typhos's fiery eyes. The burning liquid issued forth from the pinnacle of the mountain and would continue to do so every several years. Similarly, hot, violent winds would escape from the many-voiced mouths of the monster and would, even eons later, vex those at seas.

However, the volcano and the typhoon were not the only legacies left behind by Typhos for, far below the surface of the earth in a place unknown to gods and men, the children of Typhos waited, cared for by their monstrous mother Echidna and nourished on pure hate....

The stories of the gods of Mount Olympus and the many heroes, villains, and ordinary folk that they touched have remained precious commodities for the modern world. Countless scores of writers, poets, artists, inventors, and scientists have credited the myths of ancient Greece and Rome with providing for them the inspiration to create, understand, and aspire to that which might otherwise remain a mystery. The very names of the gods themselves convey elemental wonder and majesty, whether the name is bestowed upon a planetary heavenly body or the make of a brand new car. Classical mythology has endured in its everyday relevance through our language, our art, and even through our view of the cosmos.

It is easy to see why we, as a culture thousands of years removed from the days of wheat sacrifices to Demeter, are still fascinated by and study the mythology of the ancient world. Understanding the myths of a populace helps us to understand what those people were really like. The study of myth is a sort of literary archaeology allowing us to "dig" into the minds of a culture instead of just a hole in the ground. What is found there, though, is not the same as a fossil or old tools. What we find are ideological artifacts, for the development of the belief system of an ancient culture is as important to uncover as the development of a culture's land management, technology, and social system. When we understand how ancient man forged the landscape of his mind, heart, and soul, we learn not just about how he lived, but we also learn, through his perspective, why he lived.

The values of that ancient culture also become verifiable when we study myths. The role of women in myths often mirrors the role of women in the myth-culture's contemporary world. Similarly, when we see what it took to be called a "hero" in the myth-culture's world, we realize exactly what traits were held in high esteem and what foibles could cause one's immediate disgrace. Whether the stories are cautionary tales warning the audience about the dangers of angering a god or are simply lighthearted exercises in romance and adventure, the means by which good and evil, victory and defeat, or hope and despair are expressed reveal priceless treasures for our education. In many ways, reading and understanding mythology is as close to living in those ancient times as modern man will ever know.

Of course, the entertainment value of classical mythology can never be overlooked. Every area of modern day amusement has somehow been touched by the ancient world. Characters in mythology have served as templates for the heroes and tragic characters that populate books, poems, stage, and screen. Many of the plotlines of famous myths have served as the inspiration for movies, cartoons, and even soap operas. To many who study myth-cultures, it would appear that our modern mentalities are not as much sparked by myths as they are re-ignited; somehow, those characters and stories are already a part of our shared, inherent ability to make meaning, and our attraction to mythology is merely an indication that, despite differences in geography, ethnicity, or era, there is, in fact, a shared human experience.

At the core of it all, though, may be an innocent and sincere curiosity that drives us to investigate mythology. The ancient Greek and Roman craftsmen devoted an immense amount of their time and effort into constructs that paid homage to gods and goddesses or commemorated scenes of a hero's fall from grace. Cups, vases, paintings, sculptures, ornaments, and entire buildings tell tales in lavish detail and sing of deeds divine and earthly. Poets such as Hesiod, Pindar, and Ovid derived great inspiration from their era's body of myths, while the famed playwrights Aeschylus, Sophocles, and Euripides created some of the greatest tragedies of all time by tapping into the core plots of myths both popular and sublime. Why did the oral tradition of mythology so encompass the daily lives of the ancient Greeks and Romans? Why did ancient man need mythology so much?

This answer is a simple one. For ancient man, mythology equaled power. Nothing supports this assertion better than today's all too common umbrella.

Certainly, most everyone can boast of owning at least one umbrella of his or her own. Perhaps, one may even own different styles and colors of umbrellas to suit particular occasions. Whatever one's umbrella fortunes may be, it is the case that people in the modern world do not carry their umbrellas with them all the time, fearing that it might suddenly rain. The radio and television provide access to fairly reliable forecasts that can warn us several days in advance and with varying degrees of accuracy just when one might need to tote an umbrella along to work, or when not to plan an outdoor event. When we watch a news broadcast, we can even witness with our own eyes some great big blob of green on a radar map that indicates that inconvenient storm hundreds of miles away which will eventually drench our Thursday night commute home. We understand weather and we can predict it. We know when we need an umbrella, and when to toss it in the closet.

Ancient man and woman obviously did not enjoy such power. They were at the mercy of warm fronts and air masses they could not possibly understand. Rather than being continually dumbfounded by their environmental fate, they did their best to make meaning out of what was happening around them. By creating, for instance, a god of the ocean, they could give themselves some power over the all-mighty seas. Though that power might only be imaginary, it nevertheless bolstered the resolve of the people and gave them confidence that their endeavors might be all the more successful. Sacrificing a good day's catch to the god of the ocean might better ensure safe travels in their primitive vessels. We human beings are not naturally disposed to helplessness, and the ancient Greeks were certainly no exception.

The creation of a body of myths – over a long period of time and evolving as the myth-culture evolved – empowered the people of that culture in a myriad of ways. It gave them a sense of purpose, offered explanations before any science existed, and fostered a kind of collaborative ownership of the universe with the powers of nature that enabled man to push onward in the face of the gifts and curses of life.

Though the ancient Greeks and Romans derived power from their myths in many cultural as well as individual ways, the following five empowerments seem to have had the most potent and enduring impact.

Myths offered empowerment through the explanations of natural phenomena

This is the empowerment that is familiar to even the most casual readers of mythology. In order to explain everything from flash floods to rock formations to goat horns, early man's imagination did its best to fill in the gaps in his understanding. The opening myth of Typhos is a perfect example.

To explain the seething lava and explosive force of a volcano, no ordinary beast would do. The volcano was one of the most frightening elements on the landscape of ancient man's world, and the cause of such a monstrous growth upon the countryside would require a source that was as gigantic to match the volcano's size, as malevolent to rival the volcano's destructive force, and as undying and "immortal" as the volcano itself. Typhos, or Typhon, was appropriate in every way. Like a volcano, Typhos was an elemental thing, a "combination" of the under-realm of Tartarus and Mother Earth; thus, the monster was, in fact, the simultaneous expression of earth and hell – very fitting for a mountain that spews fiery venom. Like a volcano, Typhos emerged from the underground and immediately began an assault upon the land. Typhos's ability to set fire to virtually everything, even water, is consistent with the intensity of the lava which maintains its burning powers and hellish glow even when it enters the sea. His earth-tossing penchant is also consistent with the behavior of an explosive, volcanic eruption.

The volcano as an evil presence among men, however, ended there.

Empowerment over the volcano began with the plot device of Typhos's defeat. Zeus had come to the rescue of his fellow gods and engaged the monster in fierce battle. The end result of that battle was the crushing of the creature beneath Mount Aetna and, thus, the creation of the first volcano. The volcano, therefore, is not a monument to the presence of evil; rather, it is a monument to good prevailing over evil. Though the immortal beast beneath the mountain still lives and continues to create intense flames from his eyes, he no longer has the power to move about the land and menace the entire world. Typhos is effectively trapped, and his power is significantly minimized. A champion has risen and defeated an evil that had been purposefully created to triumph, and that champion, though a god, looks just like man.

Obviously, when scrutinizing the symbolic elements of the war between Typhos and Zeus, the origin of the volcano crafted by ancient man exceeds the basic need to merely understand nature. The volcano, which appears to be rising out of the earth, could have simply been a symbol of foreboding; Typhos might only be emerging in the tale as a threat for the future, rather than being fashioned as a vanquished foe in the past. The volcano, therefore, becomes a symbol of the defeat of destructive forces. Typhos is described not as an ominous doom reaching up from the earth, but as a crippled and nearly impotent perversion crushed beneath it. Through myth, man vanquishes the volcano.

A myriad of classical myths discuss the origins and explanations of natural forces. The famed Latin poet Ovid concerned himself a great deal with the subject in his Metamorphoses. Ovid used the theme of transformation to string together a multitude of stories that were popular during his time in ancient Rome. He explored how people and places were transformed by higher powers (and sometimes by their own will) into natural elements such as flowers, wind, and water, and he attempted to explain many of the fatal aspects of nature, such as volcanoes, earthquakes, and even some sicknesses, that man had come to fear. In Ovid's work, we have the basis for most of the myths with which we have become so familiar, and ancient man had the empowering explanations he so desperately needed.

Similar to the story of Typhos, the next myth to be examined features the identical objective – to explain the origin of a natural phenomenon. This story also contains a giant villain whose powers are, likewise, a hundredfold. However, the next myth contains subject matter that is far from the deadly fire spitting of a raging volcano. In fact, for such a bird as the relatively innocuous peacock, one might wonder why any explanation would be needed at all.

THE HUNDRED EYES OF ARGUS

High atop Mount Olympus, Zeus waved his hand and the clouds parted. One of the earthly groves of his wife Hera, Queen of Olympus, came clearly into view, and he pointed one mighty finger toward the lone creature tied to and lying meekly beside one of Hera's olive trees.

"Do you see her there, my son?"

Hermes scrunched up his face. "Umm, you mean the white cow?"

"Yes."

"That cow…right there?"

"Yes."

The god of roguery rubbed his boyish chin and sighed. "Okay, so you want me to rescue a cow?"

"Yes."

Hermes tried desperately not to giggle at his father's request. As the herald and messenger of the gods, Hermes knew all too well what could happen if the Great Thunderer did not receive the response that he expected. Usually, an unhappy Zeus resulted in a shower of lightning bolts upon the head of the offender. This situation, however, caused even the exceedingly clever Hermes a moment's confusion. His father had summoned him for what he had deemed "a most delicate and dangerous task," and now it appeared that the task involved the herding of a single cow.

"As always," Hermes responded to his great father, "I will do as you ask. But, I cannot help but wonder why for such a simple assignment you need - "

"Look more carefully."

Hermes' eyes returned to the scene. The heifer was indeed a magnificently delicate and attractive creature, but there did not seem to be anything more remarkable about it. Then Hermes noticed the shadow of the tree suddenly move.

The young god squinted. It was not the tree's shadow at all that was moving. Something else was lying beneath the olive tree on the side that was out of view. The obscured form moved a bit more and then walked from behind the olive tree into full view. The figure was that of an unclothed man of gigantic stature, nearly twelve feet tall. The tremendous size of the being, however, was not its most startling characteristic, for this was Argus, the watchman of Hera and the undefeated slayer of all manner of man and monster. He was by far the most recognizable warrior beast in all of the land. Argus' entire body was covered with eyes – one hundred to be exact – and because only a few of those glittering eyes needed to sleep at any one time, he was always awake and alert, and thus made the perfect guardian. Argus bore a spiked club in one hand and the tether of the cow in the other. He tugged at the rope to make sure the looped knots around the tree were continuing to hold. Satisfied that the cow was secure, the hundred-eyed giant leaned upon his club and continued his watch.

"Father, forgive the doubt that led me to dare question your wisdom. I had thought at first that this cow was nothing special. Now I see that it must be of a rare value to be guarded by Argus himself. Is it some enchanted creation of Hera? A disguised treasure? A powerful artifact?" Hermes smiled and betrayed a hint of greediness.

Zeus leaned toward his son and whispered, "It's a woman."

"A woman?" Hermes scrunched up his face again. "Oh. Okay. Not treasure. A woman. That's…uh…that's good, too."

The woman that Hermes had been so disappointed to hear about was a young maiden named Io. Her transformation into a white cow and subsequent imprisonment were nothing short of the severest embarrassment for all gods concerned with the poor maiden's plight.

The beautiful Io, daughter of the river god Inachus, had been wading by the side of one of her father's tributaries when mighty Zeus, looking down from Olympus on high, had caught sight of the maiden dangling her pretty feet in the cool water. Instantly Zeus had become enamored with Io, and he appeared before her to speak words of love into her ear. Of course, Zeus's wife Hera had grown terribly impatient with her husband's "divine visitations" to every young mortal woman of whom he had ever lain eyes, and she had become more vigilant than ever, waiting for Zeus to make one more mistake that might justify a display of anger from her the likes of which Olympus had never seen. The rage of Typhos would be a child's tantrum by comparison. To avoid that wrath, Zeus had become exceedingly careful to cover up his deeds or create some distraction, and Hera had been vexed in every instance, never able to unequivocally prove that her husband had been unfaithful again.

This time, Zeus had summoned the clouds to conceal his approach to Io, but Hera recognized the tactic. She dispelled the clouds and pointed an accusatory finger at her husband, smiling with great satisfaction as she was about to level her charges upon him. Unfortunately for the Queen of Olympus, the clearing clouds revealed only an innocent-looking Zeus standing next to an even more innocent-looking and rather stupefied white heifer, for in the time before the clouds had completely dissipated, Zeus had changed Io into a cow.

"Zeus, my lord," Hera said. "What are you doing amongst the mortals again?"

"Ah, my precious, I have been examining this lovely new animal which seems to have just recently sprung from the earth."

"My great husband, do forgive my ignorance, but is this creature not a cow? I fail to see how the word 'new' describes such a common beast."

Zeus patted Io's cow head. "But, my beloved, do you not see that this is an altogether more perfect version of the ordinary cow? Look at it! It is truly a thing of beauty! It has an exquisite bone structure…wonderfully smooth skin…a great rump."

"Of course, my husband, you would notice such things…in a cow. I offer the deepest apologies for not being more observant. Truly this is a special animal – so special, in fact, that I wish to claim it for myself."

"What?"

"Bestow this new cow to me. Consider it a gift for your beloved queen."

Io's cow eyes widened, and Zeus hesitated to reply.

Hera smiled again. "Is there some reason why I am not deserving of such a gift?"

The Great Thunderer knew that he had been bested. If he did not relinquish Io to Hera, his suspicious wife would finally have the proof of his infidelity for which she had so long been searching. Such proof might lead to awful consequences upon Mount Olympus. But poor Io was trapped in the body of a cow! Zeus could not leave the innocent girl to such a fate. Right now, though, there seemed to be nothing that he could do.

"My glorious Hera," Zeus said, "the animal is yours."

Thus, the cow became Hera's possession and was soon to be guarded by a watchman that never stopped watching and could never be passed.

For all of his might, Zeus could do nothing to betray the truth of the cow's identity. When he considered the ways in which he might enable the freedom of Io, the majority of the solutions he devised would have exposed his true motives and, thus, his guilt. Furthermore, Hera would have known what Io was and would have destroyed her – a fate the girl did not deserve. Inachus was terribly upset, having been privy to what had befallen his daughter, and he implored Zeus to do something. When Zeus considered what fellow Olympians he might entrust with the task of rescuing the innocent creature, few were truly appropriate for the job. Zeus's wandering affections would not elicit sympathy from any of the goddesses, nor would any of the gods wish to assist him for fear that their own dalliances might come to light. Zeus's son Ares, the god of war, would certainly have been a match for Argus, but Ares was also Hera's son and he was loyal to his mother. Zeus needed someone for whom subtlety and stealth were second nature. Hermes, god of thieves, traders, and cleverness itself, was the perfect choice.

Hermes accepted the assignment and soon was walking upon the earth in the guise of an old shepherd. He played upon a pipe of reeds as he walked through the garden where Io had been kept, and the sound of the music immediately caught the attention of the watchman of a hundred eyes.

"You! Shepherd!" cried Argus. "Come here!"

Hermes pretended to be apprehensive and fearful of the monster.

"I do not wish you harm," continued Argus. "I have been watching this animal for days and I am bored. Come, play your pipes for me a while."

Hermes gladly did just that. He and Argus sat beside the olive tree, and Hermes played many a tune, each one more lulling than the next. Some of Argus' bored eyes were beginning to flutter.

Realizing that music alone would not be enough to send this savage to sleep, Hermes began to tell Argus the story of how the pipe of reeds had come to be. The tale of Pan and Syrinx was a simple one. Pan was the satyr god, half man and half goat, and he chased the beautiful nymph Syrinx in the hope of catching her so that they might share a passionate moment. Syrinx wanted nothing to do with anyone who was even one-tenth goat, so she quickly fled into an outcropping of reeds where she immediately changed herself into one of the stalked foliage. Distraught Pan wished to remember his lost love by the reeds, so he fashioned a pipe out of them. It was, indeed, a simple tale, but Hermes elongated it to an extraordinary length, stretching the story to a tedious thinness and droning on in a voice that dulled the senses. Before the tale was done, most of Argus' eyes were completely closed and the ones that remained opened were drooping heavily.

To finish his task, Hermes slyly waved a wand that helped the remaining eyes close. Once Argus was fully asleep with every eyelid shut, the god of thieves unsheathed his infamous curved sword and swiftly swung the blade. The sword cut through the thick neck of Argus and bit into the olive tree, severing the rope that bound Io. In an instant, Io was free, Argus was dead, and the mysterious shepherd responsible for it all had disappeared.

When Hera came upon the scene a few hours later, she was enraged that the cow was gone, but she experienced a deeper emotion at the slaying of Argus. The stern goddess suddenly felt very sad. To immortalize the noblest and most loyal subject she had ever known, Hera took the eyes of Argus and placed them upon the feathers of her favorite bird, the peacock. That is why when a peacock fans its feathers it appears to have a multitude of glittering "eyes" all over them.

The story of the death of Argus may culminate in the release of Io, but the maiden still in cow form had much more to endure as the jealous Hera continued to torment her. After memorializing Argus, Hera summoned one of the Furies, those entities of vengeance, to drive the cow mad. The Fury relentlessly pursued the girl, never allowing her a moment's rest. The agony lasted all the way to Egypt where the people who encountered Io treated the strange white animal with awe. Zeus would eventually convince Hera that the cow could never pose any "threat" to her, and the scorned goddess, beginning to doubt that the cow was anything more than just a cow, dismissed the Fury and left the situation behind her. Io was returned to her original form and she became revered by the tribes of the Nile. She bore a son to Zeus, Epaphus, and he and all of his descendents would enjoy much favor from the Fates.

Throughout most of this myth, Hera is portrayed as justifiably suspicious and vengeful, and she becomes virtually obsessed with an animal that she is not entirely sure is the source of her shame. Deceit abounds as the goddess and her unfaithful husband engage in a game of wits in which neither will dare openly admit the true nature of the problem – as obvious as that problem may be. Not once does Hera confront Zeus with her hurt and embarrassment, and Zeus himself does nothing to alleviate his wife's pain. It is a tale that remains an excellent character study of the deities worshipped in ancient times, so long as the infidelity and the ensuing tor-ment of Io do not overshadow Hera's sincere act of compassion toward the fallen Argus.

Hera memorializes her watchman in the midst of jealously and vindic-tiveness, and is thus raised above the simplistic caricature of the scorned wife out for revenge. She takes the time to find some way to repay Argus for his service to her and for the untimely end he has met in the course of that service. Argus might only be an underling to Hera, but it is his faith-fulness and unswerving loyalty that qualify his place in the story. His death moves the goddess while she herself experiences emotional turmoil, and her response to his end creates an empowering symbol for those within the myth-culture who believed in Hera.

The peacock becomes the tangible sign of the compassion of the gods. Though their wrath might be great upon the heads of those who do them wrong, the heat of that wrath will never distract the gods from the wisdom to treat the true and the just with compassion and goodness. Furthermore, those who die in the service of their deities are blessed with the promise of a memorial; in some way they will be immortalized for their loyalty and faithfulness. The peacock, grand in appearance, empowered the people by supporting the belief that the gods were as fair and just as they were mighty and quick to punish. The feathery "eyes" offered the believer some semblance of order in an all too turbulent world.

Myths taught social and spiritual lessons of empowerment

Since a great deal of mythology formed the body of a religious belief system, it would follow that the stories most desired by those espousing the religion would be the ones that taught the followers the "right" and "wrong" of the moment. Most of the time, the gods and goddesses that were considered the major patrons of the region determined the morality of the people. There were a plethora of do-not-tick-off-the-gods myths to keep the devout from showing a lack of respect to the divine ones, and specific myths were retold regularly, usually at the same time of the year, to commemorate traditions such as harvest ceremonies or the onset of a season. The lesson taught by myths used for these purposes was always centered around remembering and respecting the gods lest they should look with disfavor on the offender and his or her family.

The spiritual elements in these learning experiences are not dissimilar to the lessons learned by the followers of every other myth-culture and religion outside of ancient Greece and Rome. It is necessary for the very survival of any belief system to have within its structure a web of myths that might be traced, strand by strand and story by story, to a center rooted in the ideal that to follow is to be saved, to be disrespectful is to be doomed. The major difference between the mythology of Greece and Rome and the mythologies of most other cultures is that spiritual lessons in classical myths were simultaneously social lessons. The true educational power of the Greek and Roman myths was not limited to merely believing in the gods – it extended to believing in one's self.

The exploration of human potential occupies more classical mythology than almost any other subject. Tales of common men swept into very uncommon situations have been among the oldest and most popular stories, surviving even those that were more spiritually based. The themes of these myths questioned life itself by presenting characters whose successes and failures were not the primary results of their interaction with the gods. Instead, responsibility for their ends rested solely at their own mortal feet. Often, the role that the gods played would be purely incidental.

That was the case with Tantalus, the renowned monarch of Phrygia. His story reveals much about how lessons of a social and spiritual nature may be interpreted by the reader of mythology.

Dinner with Tanatalus

The court of King Tantalus had not known this much excitement since the birth of the King's precious son, Pelops. Everywhere, attendants were running about wildly to complete their preparations for the festivities. Tantalus's citadel had been decorated with every delicate flower that could be plucked, and a variety of sacrifices were ready to be offered to the gods upon the benevolent monarch's return. This would surely be one of Phrygia's greatest moments!

At the appointed hour, the people readied themselves. Lines of statesmen, soldiers, and citizens crowded the citadel, but in the most honored place of all – where the cloud of Olympus itself was going to light – Pelops stood before all so that he might be the first to see his father's return.

As the last beam of sunlight disappeared beneath the mountains in the west, the cloud suddenly descended from the heavens. The silent awe of those gathered belied the hundreds that were present. All watched with reverence. This cloud was a manifestation of the gods themselves, and, more importantly, their king was at the center of it! What other kingdom could boast what the citizenry of Phrygia could? Their leader was not only an offspring of mighty Zeus, but he had also been so beloved and so honored by his divine father that he had actually been invited to dine with the gods on Mount Olympus! It was a proud moment for everyone!

The eyes of young Pelops were wide with amazement. He anxiously watched the cloud softly come to a landing on the floor of the citadel. He could not wait to see his father again.

As the essence of the cloud melted away, the figure of King Tantalus was revealed. He stood proudly, adorned in robes of royalty, and he appeared to be very happy. The instant that Tantalus saw Pelops, he ran to the boy, scooped him up in his arms, and hugged him tightly. The assemblage cheered.

"I have returned from Olympus!" announced Tantalus.

The crowd applauded.

"I have had dinner with the gods!"

The cheering and applause intensified.

"The food was really good! Loved the rolls!"

The crowd got seriously loud. Women fainted from joy. Some of the men began to weep.

Tantalus put his son Pelops down and raised his right hand to hush his enthusiastic people. He smiled broadly for he knew that his next announcement would meet with the loudest response of all.

"People of Phrygia," the King began, "I have even better news for you. Upon finishing my meal with the gods in the Great Hall of Olympus, I felt that it would have been fitting for one treated as well as I had been treated to repay wondrous Zeus, perfect Hera, and all of the other great ones by offering to host a meal for them in my own home. I did not expect the gods to accept such a humble invitation…but they have! People of Phrygia, one month from this day, the gods will be coming here for dinner!"

The crowd was a mass of gleeful hysteria. Pelops wrapped his arms around his father's waist, and Tantalus patted the boy's head.

"Oh, my son!" Tantalus cried. "We are blessed! The dinner will be magnificent! When the gods come to Phrygia, would you like to be at the table with them?"

The boy cheered as loudly as any spectator. "Yes, Father! Yes!"

"Then you shall, my boy!"

And so, the new preparations began. The planning would encompass all of their days and nights for the next month, but the people knew that there could be no better way to spend their time than by making certain this unprecedented reception was the best it could be. Tantalus was no less excited than his people and he agonized over the menu for nearly the entire duration.

One month later, all was ready. This time, the attendants had done much in advance, and no one ran wildly about. All adhered to a strict code of reverence. They had planned well.

Tantalus stood in the same place that his son had been standing when the child had waited for the King's return. Now, he felt the same anxious thrill that his son had felt one month before. It was glorious!

Another cloud descended from the heavens. When it dissipated, there stood the Olympians in full grandeur. Zeus, Hera, Demeter, Poseidon, Hestia, Hephaestus, Ares, Athena, Apollo, Artemis, Hermes, and Dionysus were miraculously present in the citadel of Tantalus. Hades, lord of the dead, had remained in the Underworld to tend to the souls of the just and to torment the souls of the wicked.

Tantalus bowed. "Welcome, Father Zeus! Welcome gods of Olympus! I have the most special meal prepared for you!"

The gods took their places at Tantalus's table. The King had relinquished the head of the table to Zeus and occupied the other end. He waited until all of the gods had been seated before he took his place. To all who witnessed the awesome gathering, the gods appeared benevolent, friendly, and the worthiest of guests.

With a clap of his hands, Tantalus signaled for the dinner to be served. Attendants quickly obeyed the summons and, as they had practiced for weeks, presented the steaming bowls of stew to each god simultaneously. The Olympians were eager to try this mortal meal and looked upon the dish with much curiosity.

None, though, would touch the food. For a moment, the gods exchanged glances that betrayed serious concern. Tantalus looked about, worried. Then all turned toward the head of the table to wait for some sign from Zeus.

Zeus's piercing eyes met the eyes of his host. "Is this dish what I think it is?"

Tantalus swallowed hard. "I would never presume to know what you are thinking, Father Zeus. But I can tell you it is a stew made of the most rare and priceless ingredients that Phrygia has to offer."

"Rare?" muttered Zeus. "Priceless?"

"Yes," responded Tantalus. "Most definitely."

Thunder erupted within the citadel, and fierce bolts of lightning danced across the ceiling. "You foul beast!" roared Zeus. "The meat in this stew is your own son Pelops! You slaughtered your son!"

"Unthinkable!" exclaimed Demeter.

"Disgusting!" cried Dionysus.

Tantalus cringed in his chair. "But...I thought you..."

"Grant me your permission, Zeus," said Ares, god of war. "I will gladly summon an army of marauders to lay waste to this monster's kingdom and all his people!"

"No, my son! We shall leave the fate of this creature that I am ashamed to call my own offspring to Hades and his creative punishments. For now, we will attend to Pelops."

"The child must be restored," said Hestia, goddess of the hearth. "Let us combine our divinity and return this wronged being to life."

Hermes snickered. "Hades will not be happy to have the soul taken back from him."

"Do not worry," Zeus said to Hermes as he glanced toward Tantalus. "He will have a new one to play with very soon."

The gods clasped their hands together and a blinding light filled the dining hall. When the light had cleared, Pelops was back and looked as alive as ever. The only lasting effect of the horror he had suffered at the hands of his own father was that one of his shoulder bones had not been returned to his reformed body. The gods quickly amended this with a new bone of pure ivory.

The gifts of the gods did not end there. Every Olympian present bestowed something of great value to Pelops to make up for the act that they felt their presence had somehow precipitated. Poseidon, lord of the sea, took a special interest in the boy and promised he would always be there for him, vowing to do what he could to help Pelops earn a kingdom of his own.

As for Tantalus, the attentions of the gods were far less benevolent. The former King of Phrygia was immediately given to Hades in the Underworld. Hades was glad to receive a replacement for the soul of Pelops, but even the gloomy lord of the dead who lived among miseries all the time was disturbed by Tantalus's abominable deed. To the satisfaction of the rest of the gods, Hades arranged for the punishment of Tantalus to truly fit the crime.

Food and drink would be Tantalus's torment. For all eternity, he would suffer from unceasing and painful hunger and thirst. Worse than that, Tantalus would remain fixed to one spot while wading up to his neck in clean, clear water. Just next to his mouth would be the branch of a tree bearing the most delicious and succulent fruit. If ever Tantalus tried to bow his head to drink, the water would instantly recede. Similarly, when he tried to snatch a piece of fruit, the branch would quickly move out of his reach. Forever and ever, the disgraced King of Phrygia would be "tantalized" by the fruit and water, but would never be satisfied. He would know only the agonies of hunger and thirst and the realization that this punishment and the loss of his wealth, power, renown, and freedom were entirely his own fault.

Missing from the story of Tantalus is an explanation of the motive behind the slaying of Pelops. What caused a man of such high esteem to commit an act as base as the cannibalization of his own son? Most of the ancient poets do not give reasons for Tantalus's ghastly behavior, but often they cite his fitting punishment in the Underworld because of its clever appropriateness. It is that punishment and its connection to the word "tantalize" that has kept this myth alive for so many centuries.

So, why did Tantalus do it? Some versions of the myth ascribe excessive pride to the nature of Tantalus. Since he had enjoyed the favor of the gods in such a public manner, the honor had caused him to perceive himself as godlike. Taking the life of his son as part of a ceremonial sacrifice might have been his attempt to feel more like a god.

Other versions tell of a Tantalus so overwhelmed by his meal with the gods that his vanity clouded his judgment. With an ego dangerously swelled, Tantalus wanted to test the gods to see if their powers were as great as everyone believed. Having joined them in the Great Hall of Olympus must have made them seem less godly and more human to Tantalus, and perhaps he wanted to establish if they were as divine as all the faithful claimed.

There are some versions that actually take a more forgiving look at Tantalus's deed. In these stories, Tantalus has offered his son to the gods as the ultimate act of personal sacrifice. In his sincere but shortsighted attempt to show devotion to the gods, he presents something that is genuinely special to him in the hope that they will be impressed by his unselfishness.

No matter the version, the outcome is always the same – and that is important. The punishment of Tantalus forms the basis for the social and spiritual lessons to be learned.

The social leeson begins with the idea that Tantalus has been blessed with a life of remarkable fortune. He was a god-sired king among mortals, wealthy and powerful. He was beloved by his people and his family, and he had been favored by heaven itself. Rare were kings so respected, and even rarer were kings that could prove a connection to the Almighty. Certainly, this was a man that other men might wish to become. The majority of men and women in ancient times, however, had little chance of experiencing even a fraction of the privilege enjoyed by Tantalus. Thus, the fate of the once-great King of Phrygia stands as an empowering equalizer to the people of ancient times. If a man like Tantalus was not exempt from the wrath of the gods, than there was justice in the universe after all.

In fact, so many of the myths that deal with punishment involve kings who lose everything because of their own foolishness or disrespect for the gods. Everyone knows of King Midas, the man whose wish to make golden all that he touched led to his near death by starvation. Then there was clever King Sisyphus, a master trickster and fraud who was punished with the eternal task of pushing a rock up a hill, only to have it roll back down to the bottom before he ever made it to the top. King Ixion of the Lapithae of Thessaly had been responsible for many misdeeds born of his lust, and he remains tied to a wheel that rolls along an endless road in the Underworld. Dozens of other monarchs are detailed in the myths of ancient Greece and Rome, and all of the ones who behave in a foul manner pay for their sins. For the ancient societies that believed in these myths, there were no special privileges for those who wore a crown; the gods looked upon everyone equally, no matter his or her station in life.

The spiritual lesson conveyed through the story of Tantalus is also one that is common among the myths of its time. No one is exempt from showing the proper respect to the gods or to their fellow mortals, not even one who is of Zeus's own divine blood. The wrath of the Olympians is swift and just. More importantly, the gods are not concerned with the motive for the deed; the act that is committed is what they judge. Perhaps that is why the earliest references to Tantalus do not provide a suitable explanation for why he uses his son as the secret ingredient to his stew. In essence, the reason does not matter. There is no mercy for those who "made an honest mistake" or "meant well." The rules of the cosmos were known to all, and every mortal was expected to follow those laws or be punished, no matter the reason for the deed.

In the myths that appear here and in other sources, the reader will see time and again how characters with great potential achieve wondrous things when they are good to themselves, kind to others, respectful of the gods, and carefully consider the consequences of all of their actions. Characters who began their lives with little or nothing could follow these guidelines and enjoy many, many years filled with prosperity. It was the same for the ancient audiences of these myths as well. The common man or woman could learn the lessons and follow the guidelines and be as

happy and fulfilled as the noblest king. These were the lessons and guidelines that not only aided the daily lives of the shepherd or the farmer or
the fisherman, but also fostered an entire civilization to greatness.

Myths were attempts to explore and understand conflicts that had yet to be resolved

Though today's science, technology, and medicine have solved many of
the physical problems that have plagued humanity, men and women are
still not immune to the emotional aspects of existence that continue to
defy resolution. Perhaps those issues, like love and loss, are easier now to
manage because less of the universe is a mystery, but, for ancient man to
whom all was obscure, the emotional and physical conflicts that had yet to
be resolved were resoundingly intimidating.

In order to cope with these difficulties, ancient man began telling
myths that attempted to resolve those problems, offering some hope or
consolation through a divine solution. When the solution was not divine,
it was at least faith-based or mystical. The modern day reader of mythology, whose eyes have been opened to many of the mysteries of existence,
does not readily see the hope or consolation residing in the tale; sometimes, the reader even fails to identify what the central conflict really is.
When readers miss that element of the story, the true power of the myth
has eluded them.

Because mythology's roots are based in the oral tradition, no one definitive version of any single myth exists; multiple variations abound. This is
actually more of an advantage than a hindrance to today's readers of myth.
One of the easiest ways for a modern day reader to extract the central conflict that the myth is attempting to solve is to read more than one version
of the same story. The social anthropologist Claude Lévi-Strauss first for-
mally suggested this clever technique in his essay "The Structural Study of
Myth." When comparing different versions, the reader ought to focus

attention on the elements that are similar rather than be distracted by the differences. Within those similarities lies the truth.

To illustrate, what follows are two versions of the myth of Endymion. The major difference between each is the identity of the goddess who falls in love with the mortal Endymion. That difference will serve to distinguish the two stories in the proceeding discussion.

ENDYMION (ARTEMIS VARIANT)

Artemis, the daughter of Zeus, was the goddess of the moon and the hunt. She was also the special patroness of all maidens. Like her twin brother Apollo, Artemis was charged with the task of guiding the movement of the heavens. While her brother drove the Chariot of the Sun, she was responsible for the Chariot of the Moon and the golden hinds that pulled it. Never did she waver in her duties, except for the time when she met Endymion.

One night, as the silver chariot of the moon passed over the fields of Mount Latmos, Artemis spied a handsome young shepherd named Endymion asleep in the soft grass. The shepherd's beauty awed the goddess, a first for young Artemis. Never before had a god or a mortal had any effect on her heart. Even when the handsomest of gods had professed love, Artemis rebuffed the proposal. She was, after all, the one to whom maidens prayed; she had to remain chaste, and it had been easy to do so…until now.

For several nights, Artemis passed Mount Latmos and merely watched the young man as he slept amid his flock, but her desire to be with him grew until she could deny it no more. Eventually, she decided to visit Endymion in his dreams. In that way, she would remain a maiden, but still have some contact with him. Upon their first dream-meeting, the two fell deeply in love.

Unfortunately, while Artemis visited Endymion in his dreams, she was ignoring the reins of the Chariot of the Moon. Without her hand, the golden hinds would wander around the heavens, sometimes chasing falling stars, sometimes just sitting in one place. Very soon, all of the inhabitants of earth and Olympus took notice of the erratic movements of the moon.

Zeus summoned his daughter before him. When Artemis told him of the cause of her negligence, the Great Thunderer was moved to pity rather than anger. Having himself fallen in love with mortals, he knew of the great pain it would cause his daughter to watch Endymion grow old and die. At the same time, he was also proud to see that Artemis had maintained her status as patroness of maidens by visiting Endymion in his sleep. That tactic gave Zeus an idea.

Zeus placed Endymion in an eternal sleep. He would never age and never die, but he would never waken either. The goddess of the moon could then visit him during the day in his dreams. In this way, the love of Artemis and Endymion would never die.

ENDYMION (SELENE VARIANT)

Selene, the daughter of the Titan Hyperion, was the goddess of the moon. Like her brother Helios, Selene was charged with the task of guiding the movement of the heavens. While her brother drove the Chariot of the Sun, she was responsible for the Chariot of the Moon and the white horses that pulled it. Never did she waver in her duties, except for the time when she met Endymion.

One night, as the silver chariot of the moon passed over the fields of Mount Latmos, Selene spied a handsome young shepherd named Endymion asleep in the soft grass. The shepherd's beauty awed the goddess, a first for young Selene. Never before had a god or a mortal had any effect on her heart. Even when the handsomest of gods had professed love, Selene rebuffed the proposal. That night, Selene returned her white horses late to their stables, nearly upsetting the balance of the heavens. She had been staring at Endymion for quite some time, causing that night to be longer than it ought to have been.

Not knowing what to do, Selene went to her sister, Eos, goddess of the dawn. Having herself fallen in love with a mortal, Eos knew of the great pain it would cause her sister to watch Endymion grow old and die. Changing Endymion into an immortal was not always best, for he might still age just like Eos's husband Tithonus had years before. Poor Tithonus had withered away before Eos's eyes, eventually aging all the way into a grasshopper. Selene did not want this for Endymion. Together, she and Selene came upon a solution.

Selene placed Endymion in an eternal sleep. He would never age and never die, but he would never waken either. The goddess of the moon could then visit him during the day while he slept. As Endymion dreamed of loving the most beautiful woman he had ever "seen," he would never realize that she was truly there with him. Thus, the love of Selene and Endymion would never die. To Endymion, Selene bore fifty daughters.

The differences between these two versions of the same myth are quite significant, but the universal conflict being resolved is identical. For the modern day reader to truly understand that central conflict and grasp the inherent hope of the story, it is helpful to examine both versions because of those differences. If one was to read only the Artemis variant, one might become distracted by the characterization of Zeus as a sympathetic father. The reader might also inflate the importance of the virginity of Artemis beyond what is necessary. In the Selene variant, one might be distracted by the potential victim status of the totally unaware young man who is never even consulted about his own fate. When these versions of the myth are side by side and a careful reader expels the differences and focuses on the similarities, the power of the myth becomes clear.

An immortal goddess has fallen in love with a mortal man. The goddess is representative of the moon, that heavenly body which often is used as a symbol of romance. The goddess might choose to only love her mortal from afar, but the ache to be with him is stronger than the will to keep her distance. However, of all the obstacles that hinder the couple's together-ness, it is mortality that offers the greatest threat to their happiness. The solution to the death of love lies in sleep. If the mortal sleeps forever, never aging but never waking, than the immortal may join him any time she pleases. Love will last forever.

The Endymion myth is an attempt to affirm the hope that love can be everlasting. Lovers of all ages pledge their hearts to one another for all eter-nity. Unfortunately, mortality ruins the possibility of actually being together longer than one's own natural lifespan. Love's beauty is thus tainted by the looming specter of death. Thankfully, the fate of Endymion leaves lovers some possibility that their bonds to one another might just remain secure for all time.

Of course, the hope or consolation offered to mortal lovers by the Endymion myth might be fleeting at best because the central conflict cannot be resolved so easily in real life. Nevertheless, it is a story that has stirred the hearts of men and women for centuries. It has been the inspiration for a number of poets and lyricists from ancient to modern times, and many works of literature allude to Endymion's sleep as the unending continuance of love. Today's readers must remember that the power of the myth is not found in a practical solution to mortality, but rather in its romantic and magical treatment of the subject. The harsh reality remains – there is no solution to mortality, but faith can ease the anxiety.

Often, that is all a myth of this type can do. Examine the Artemis variant again. By utilizing familiar and powerful symbolic figures like Artemis, Zeus, the Chariot of the Moon, and the golden hinds, the story is rooted in an already established belief system. The addition of a common man, in this case a shepherd rather than a king, enables the largest segment of the myth-culture's population to easily relate to the main character and the conflict. Finally, a solution to the unsolvable is presented, and the tale ends on a happy note. The more faith the audience members have, the happier the story will make them.

So, for every emotional or psychological conflict that torments mankind, there is at least one myth that explores and attempts to solve that problem. The solutions may not be realistic, but humans are always trying to do something that will improve the quality of life. While we wait for the discoveries that will someday solve all of our problems, the telling of myths has been and continues to be a wonderfully heartening way to pass the time.

Myths personified abstractions that ancient man could not comprehend

Ancient man had few problems coping with tangible enemies. A club or spear wielded in just the right manner reconciled troublesome issues and ensured that an offender would pose no threat ever again. Often, the enemies that had been successfully defeated defined entire segments of a population.

The most irksome enemy of humanity, though, is the intangible one. Ancient man, still struggling with so many mysteries of his environment, was most vulnerable to the assaults of that which could not be seen or understood easily. The intangible enemies such as disease, calamity, and strife could not be bludgeoned away or threatened out of existence; they were perpetual enemies that made the earliest civilizations feel helpless – and humanity does not like to feel helpless.

It became necessary, whether upon a whim or by design, to give "bodies" to the phantom enemies that stalked the people, to rationalize the intangible. Stories began to evolve about the forces that worked to harm the good of mankind. The elements of nature, known to lash out with a fury against which none could defend, were given names so that they might at least be cursed when they assaulted the innocent. Though man might yet remain the victim of plague and famine and drought, he could at least show some defiance.

Most likely, this was the true "birth" of the gods. Since nature could be both benevolent and destructive, a "personality" could be ascribed to the element. Consider the duality of water. Without water, there can be no life, human or otherwise, but when there is too much water on the land, as in the case of a massive flood, many lives can be lost. Each of the major gods in the Greek pantheon has had some relation to an element of nature, and each of those gods has exhibited both kindness as well as cruelty. Zeus represented thunder and lightning. Poseidon was the god of the seas. Demeter was the goddess of the harvest. The others were similarly representative of some aspect of the natural world, and all had their good moods as well as their bad.

Over time, though, the personalities of the gods became much more complex. Stories that were passed on from generation to generation became more elaborate, and, as different cultures met and shared their mythologies, the gods became fleshed out and as real as the storytellers themselves. Soon, the element that alternately helped and hurt mankind was one that could be reasoned with through prayer, sacrifice, and devotion. Man believed that through faith he could have some sort of control over nature.

Not every intangible was so easily rationalized into deification. There could be no reconciliation with those entities that were purely harmful. They remained as things to be named and despised. In Hesiod's Theogony, the ancient Greek poet personifies such fiends as Doom, Misery, Resentment, Deceit, and Old Age. Personification was a common practice among the mythmakers of the ancient world. No greatness in story or song was ever attributed to these beings, but often they appeared in tales in their personified forms so that gods and heroes might challenge and defeat them. People loved to hear stories in which Disease was thrown into a pit, or Strife was slain in battle. Such myths offered comfort to the listener and propagated the notion that man could triumph over anything.

In the following myth, made popular by the playwright Euripides, the famed hero Hercules grapples with the most hated intangible enemy of them all. This story was a favorite in ancient times and extended empowerment to the people in a most obvious way.

THE FIGHT FOR ALCESTIS

The city-state of Pherae in the land of Thessaly was a welcomed sight to Hercules, son of Zeus. Long had he traveled, and his previous labor, the capturing of the mammoth Cretan bull, was now a thing of the past. He was presently on his way to Thrace where his eighth impossible labor, the breaking of the man-eating mares of Diomedes, awaited him. He would need to rest and find shelter before continuing on, though, and Pherae was the perfect place for such a respite. Here he would find the home of his old friend Admetus, King of Pherae, and that meant the evening was certain to be one filled with wine, merry-making, and song.

Through the gates of the palace of Admetus, Hercules entered unchecked. No guard or citizen was on hand to establish the identity of those passing through the royal entrance, and the son of Zeus thought this strange. He wondered about this most seriously. Then the thoughts of the mighty Hercules turned to a funny story that he would love to tell at Admetus's table this evening, and he quickly forgot about the unguarded gates, slung his club over his shoulder, and proceeded into the king's abode.

"Admetus!" Hercules called out. "Come host the slayer of the Hydra and regale in his most funny story!"

A servant, drawn in face and dressed in black, emerged from an alcove and addressed the visitor with the utmost respect. "Great Hercules," said the servant, "my master and king is presently occupied with a matter most grievous. If it pleases you to wait momentarily, I will tell him of your arrival."

"My thanks, good citizen," answered Hercules. "Tell me, what is it that occupies the kingdom so?"

The servant did not make eye contact with Hercules. He turned on his heels and brusquely left the room, saying, "I will find King Admetus for you."

Hercules scratched his beard and wondered about the servant's strange behavior, but then he remembered all the frivolity of his last visit to Pherae, and the odd servant was soon forgotten.

Much time had passed before King Admetus arrived. The King was not adorned in his customary robes of red and gold. The robes he now wore were the very darkness of mourning – funereal robes most somber. Despite the drab attire, the King extended his hand warmly to his guest and summoned the energy to offer Hercules a friendly smile.

"Good Hercules! Brave ancestor of Perseus himself! Welcome to my home!" The King embraced his friend, but the hug was much weaker than normal.

Hercules grasped the King by the shoulders and looked at the pallor of his face. "Admetus...your face...your robes. What has befallen the kingdom? Are your children well?"

"Yes, my friend. They are fine. Do not concern yourself with my appearance. You are my guest, and, as your host, I cannot allow you even a moment's grief."

"Bah! There is grimness about. Who has died?"

Admetus averted his gaze. "A stranger. That is all. I wear the robes, as is custom. Please, think nothing of it. Tell me, bold Hercules, what brings you to Pherae?"

"I am on my way to Thrace. The journey is long, so I thought to spend the night here, but there seems to be something going on. Maybe I should find somewhere else to stay. I do not want to impose."

"No!" cried Admetus. "I say again do not concern yourself with the sad affairs of the state. I insist that you remain here tonight, as is your pleasure.

All that is mine is yours, old friend. Eat and drink until you are content, and it will be my honor to have all of your needs and comforts met."

Hercules placed a brawny arm around the shoulders of the King. "Ah, Admetus! My thanks a million times! It will be good to dine in your hall once more – a blessing before I wrestle with the fiendish stables of Diomedes! And, I have for you quite the dinner treat – a saucy tale about a naughty water nymph and three sailors! Ha, ha, ha!" Hercules laughed heartily, then suddenly turned quite serious. "Wait. You haven't heard that one yet, have you?"

"No."

"Good! Ha, ha, ha!"

The hour upon which dinner was served found Hercules alone at the banquet table in the King's dining hall, but many servants were present and attended to the hero's every need. The wine was offered as quickly as the son of Zeus could drink it, and soon the great Hercules was alternating between singing bawdy songs about nymphs of all sorts and bellowing aloud for the company of King Admetus. The servants shunned the eyes of the sole dinner guest and left food and drink before him, never addressing the questions posed to them about their master.

"Ah, good wine!" slurred Hercules. "Where is Admetus? Where is my host? You there, tell me where is – Oh, is that lamb?"

The servants kept up with the frenetic pace of the mighty one and avoided his questions, but Hercules was not the easiest guest to entertain.

"Who will sing a song with me?" shouted Hercules. "I want to sing a song about…about…I don't remember the song. Wait! Hold on! I think it was about a naughty nymph! Yes! That's it! Who will sing with me? You there!"

The servant to whom Hercules pointed cringed in fear. He tried to slink out of the room, but the son of Zeus grabbed him by the front of his robes and lifted him up.

"You will sing with me!"

"Uh, I…um…"

"Oh, there was a nymph of Mount Pelion, a nymph who loved to – you're not singing!"

"I'm sorry, Master Hercules," the young man muttered while quivering.

Hercules shook the servant roughly. "What is going on here? Tell me now, and lie at your own peril! These hands that crushed the throat of the Nemean lion will do far worse to your puny bones. Where is Admetus?"

"He is in mourning," the servant stammered. "He is at the funeral."

"But this is the funeral of a stranger!"

"No, Master Hercules. It is no stranger. The King did not want to dishonor himself as your host by upsetting you with the truth."

Hercules lowered the servant into a chair. "Tell me the truth or suffer. Who has died?"

The servant's eyes filled with tears. "The Queen is dead! The wife of King Admetus, our beautiful Queen Alcestis, is dead!"

"What? Alcestis? No!" Hercules scowled. "Take me to King Admetus, now."

In no time, the servant had shown Hercules to the funeral parlor where Admetus sat in mourning. The hero bashed the doors of the parlor open with a single swing of his enormous club and stormed inside, roughly pushing attendants and mourners out of his way. Though the behavior of Hercules was highly offensive and insensitive, none protested aloud, fearful of Hercules' notorious rage.

"Admetus! Why have you kept this from me?" Hercules pointed at the pale, unmoving body of beautiful Queen Alcestis lying upon the sacred altar.

"I know of your labors, Hercules," Admetus answered. "You are atoning for the death of your own wife and children. It would have been wrong for me to burden you with this sort of grief. Alcestis would not have wanted me to do that."

"Alcestis..." Hercules looked more closely at the face of the Queen and he realized how abominably thoughtless his behavior had been. Here was Alcestis, still young – a woman who should have been many years from death – yet she was adorned in funereal robes and was displayed for all the mourners to see. She was dead, and all Hercules had cared about was his own perceived mistreatment.

The son of Zeus began to weep. "I am sorry for the way I have acted. My temper…sometimes, I cannot control it."

"Do not worry, Hercules," said Admetus. "Your shame cannot compare to my own."

"Your shame? I do not understand. What has happened here, Admetus?"

The King's eyes filled with tears. "It is my fault, Hercules. It is my fault that my wife's soul will be lost. I should have been the one on that funeral altar, not Alcestis. Listen to my story.

"Many years ago, your half-brother, the great god Apollo, had been punished by Zeus and was made my slave for a term of one year. Apollo had been angered when Zeus killed his son, Phaëthon, but then his wrath was unquenchable when Zeus struck down his other son, Asclepius. Asclepius was a healer of extraordinary abilities, taught by his divine father himself. He had become so proficient in his arts that he was able to stave off death inevitably. Terrible Hades felt wronged by Asclepius because the healer was too good at what he did, and the lord of the Underworld was no longer receiving souls into his domain. Hades convinced Zeus that Asclepius might well aspire to becoming godlike, and Zeus agreed that such powers over life and death belonged only to the purest of immortals. He struck down Asclepius, killing the beneficent healer instantly. Thus, Apollo had been bereft of two sons by the thunderbolts of almighty Zeus. Enraged, Apollo took hold of his silver bow and arrows and avenged his sons by slaying the Cyclopes, the makers of Zeus's thunder and lightning. Apollo paid for this act of defiance by becoming my slave.

"I knew well that I had the authority of Zeus behind me. I could have worsened the punishment of Apollo in any way that I saw fit, but I also knew that at the end of the year, Apollo would be free to return to me any abuse that I might have heaped upon him. Besides, I held no malice toward him and liked him very much. I gave Apollo charge of my flocks. He did a wondrous job as a shepherd and he filled the valley with the sweetest of music. Often, I spent time with him just to listen to him play his lyre. It was magnificent.

"When I fell in love with Admetus, the daughter of King Pelias of Iolcus in Thessaly, I would have surely had no chance of winning her hand from that crafty King if not for Apollo's aid. Pelias would only give Admetus to the suitor who could ride into Iolcus in a chariot drawn by boars and lions, an impossible task. Of course, nothing is impossible for a god, and Apollo was able to tame the animals into submission. I rode proudly into Pelias's city, and he had no choice but to comply with his own order.

"Alcestis and I were so happy together. We were blessed with beautiful children. Our kingdom flourished. Apollo regularly visited us, and we were equally happy when you, my good friend, passed through our city and stayed as our guest. The Fates, however, were not so kind.

"Recently, I became ill. No one, except perhaps the long deceased Asclepius, could help me. I was dying even though I thought I would have enjoyed many more years on this earth. Apollo came to me, but even he did not have the power alone to return life to me. He went to Hades on my behalf to beseech him to return my life, but the lord of the dead would not be denied a soul, especially not by Apollo. He had still not forgotten the 'meddling' of Asclepius, Apollo's son. Hades, however, had been moved by Apollo's powerful words, and a deal was struck. If another person would volunteer to die for me, then I would survive my illness and live a long life.

"Apollo first went to my loyal subjects, all of whom had said so often and with apparent passion that they would die for their King. None, though, would volunteer to take my place. He then went to my parents, both elderly and near their ends. They too cherished their lives, even the little that was left. It was Alcestis, my precious Queen, who came forward to take my place. Apollo tried to talk her out of it, hoping there was another solution, but she was insistent. The deal was made, and, to my shame, when I heard of it, I did not protest; I loved my own life as much as I loved Alcestis. She received my illness, and I recovered. Angry with me, Apollo left.

"And now she lays here dying, and my grief devours me more than the illness had." The King sobbed loudly. "What kind of a man am I, Hercules? How could I let this happen?"

Hercules pounded his club. "Wait! She is dying, you say – not dead? That dark thief Death has not taken her yet?"

Admetus shook his head. "My advisors say that the illness will claim her very soon."

"No!" cried Hercules. "Death will not take such a caring creature! Hercules will not allow it!"

No sooner had Hercules bellowed with resignation than the shadowy figure of Death floated into the parlor. Few could see the fiend, but all could feel its chilly presence. As Death approached Alcestis, the Queen's pale face grew a ghastly white. Hercules noticed the change in the Queen's face and he immediately spun around to find the cause. He was able to just barely discern the black, ghostly creature as it reached out for Alcestis's soul.

"Villain!" shouted Hercules. "Face me and be defeated!"

Hercules charged after Death and clung on to the fiend with all of his might. Death tried to pass through the grip of mighty Hercules, but the son of Zeus was too strong. Hercules was wrestling Death successfully.

The specter reached out to place its icy hands on the body of the hero, perhaps to take his life as well, but all of Death's efforts were for nothing. Hercules smashed Death into the wall numerous times and pummeled the fiend with punches that could have shattered the pillars of the strongest palace. Never having suffered such a painful thrashing, Death forgot about Alcestis and worried about itself. As quickly as it could escape Hercules' fists, it floated out of the parlor, vowing to stay away from Alcestis and Admetus for a very long time.

Immediately, the color returned to Alcestis's cheeks, and she sat up looking as healthy as ever. Her children rushed to her and threw their arms around her. Alcestis then reached out her hand to her husband.

Admetus held down his head. "I am ashamed that I was willing to let you die for me."

"Do not be ashamed to love life," Alcestis told her husband. "There was nothing you could have said or done to have changed my mind. Your people and your children needed you. I needed you, and there would have been no life for me if you were not in it."

The King and Queen embraced, and all of the mourners became celebrants of a most wondrous occasion. Today there would be a feast in Pherae, and the guest of honor had not only accomplished an incredible feat, but he was also very ready to tell a tale about a naughty water nymph and three sailors to anyone who would listen.

The abstraction called "Death" in the story of Alcestis is a separate being from the god of the dead, Hades. It was necessary in ancient times to have someone like Hades, as grim as he was, to appeal to when circumstances arose in which some hope or some consolation might be found. Yet, people were aware of the inexorable "will" of death, and such a single-minded entity needed to exist to account for the fated death that awaited all. The character of Hades had become far too complex to be reduced to an elemental force, so death itself was personified, just as other abstractions like Terror and Destruction had been.

Hercules' success over Death aided in the belief that the will of a hero can be even stronger than the relentless will of Death. Through the personification and subsequent beating of Death, the myth was a reminder to all of the potential of mankind. If a person is great enough, he or she can accomplish anything. This was the empowerment that drove the greatness of the Hellenic Age.

Myths entertained the populace when no other entertainment existed

Sometimes, the symbolic depth of a myth was miniscule compared to the entertainment value it carried in its telling and retelling. Stories only survived the oral tradition if they were valuable, and that value could take many forms. A myth that was purely entertaining was as important to an ancient culture as one that taught a lesson or furthered a religious belief.

Myths also served as the foundations for innumerable dramas. The audience was already familiar with the characters in mythology, so a prior connection existed. The dramatist needed only to give words to the actors who would then bring those characters to life on the stage, much to the delight of the audience.

Many myths remained alive throughout the centuries because they were fun stories to experience again and again. The story of Melampus is a good example of this. Though the story is related to the famous myth of Perseus through its setting and the character of Acrisios, the grandfather of Perseus, Melampus's tale stands on its own. In this minor myth, there are no cataclysmic battles, no terrible monsters, and the "hero" is quite unconventional when compared to other heroic characters in classical mythology. Nevertheless, its charming, fable-like qualities and its general appeal have kept this myth alive for a very long time.

MELAMPUS AND THE COW GIRLS

King Proetus of Argos felt that he was always struggling, no matter what he was trying to do. From childhood, he had fought with his older brother Acrisios over every trivial thing. It did not matter what the situation involved; there was always a fight. When it came time for the brothers to decide who would rule the city-state of Argos, it came as no surprise to anyone that there would be more struggles between these two mortal enemies, possibly even a civil war. In every confrontation, Acrisios bested Proetus every time, and it appeared that poor Proetus would never be fulfilled in his quest for what he believed he deserved. Luckily for Proetus, Acrisios experienced a bad turn when an oracle had given him a very unfavorable prediction. Out of fear for what the oracle had told him, Acrisios retreated into his citadel at Larisa. Proetus seized the opportunity to attack and, with the help of his wife's relatives in the Lycian court, he was easily triumphant. Reigning from his own citadel in Tiryns, Proetus became King of Argos, and all appeared to be going well for the new sovereign.

Then, his daughters started mooing.

Early one morning and for no apparent reason, King Proetus's three beautiful daughters were found in the royal fields standing about with the cows. They were dressed in the same bedclothes they had been wearing the previous night, but they certainly were not acting the same way. The girls were grazing on the grass, following the herd, and occasionally mooing very loudly. Though they looked as normal as ever, they were clearly behaving like the very bovine around them.

Proetus was beside himself. Here was yet another struggle with which to contend. He went to his daughters to try to talk some sense into them, but it was to no avail; the King might very well have been speaking to real cows. Unsure as to what to do next, King Proetus summoned every wise man in Argos and Lycia to come to his aid in the hope that someone would know what to do. Many tried to understand the strange affliction that had driven the girls to believe themselves cows, but none of the advisors could fathom the bizarre circumstance. At times, it appeared that the girls were actually trying to moo something to the people around them, but no one could comprehend the sounds. However, some of the advisors had heard of a man who might be able to understand what the girls were saying. His name was Melampus.

When Melampus was a young man, he had saved two baby snakes that had lost their mother. While others would have killed the snakes, Melampus cared for them and reared them with a nurturing touch. The grateful creatures slithered into Melampus's ears one night and licked them clean. So clear was his hearing the next day that Melampus was able to understand the speech of all manner of animals, birds, and insects. Though he could not speak to the animals, he could eavesdrop on their every word, and the secrets of nature became his to use in the caring and nurturing of everyone and everything. Over the years, Melampus became one of the most renowned soothsayers in all of Greece. He was offered much compensation for the wonderful work that he alone could do.

Proetus sent for Melampus at once. When the soothsayer arrived, the King described to him all that had befallen his daughters in the past few days. Melampus listened carefully to the story, and a grave look came over his face. He told the King that he had a suspicion about what had happened, and he believed that listening to the girls and healing them would be one of the most dangerous assignments he had ever taken. Therefore, his fee for this task would be one-third of Proetus's kingdom.

Proetus flatly refused the charge. After struggling as he had against Acrisios just to win Argos, he was not about to give any part of it away to a perfect stranger. King Proetus dismissed Melampus immediately.

The girls grew worse during the next few days. They were filthy and sickly; they refused regular food, preferring to graze with the herd, but the grass they were eating was making them ill. The King's advisors were certain that his daughters would not live much longer under these conditions. It seemed that he had no choice but to accept Melampus's terms.

When the King summoned the soothsayer once more, Melampus had changed his mind. Now he was asking for one-third of the kingdom for himself and another one-third for his brother. Reluctantly, Proetus agreed.

Melampus and several citizens of Argos went out to capture the girls. The task was not easy, for the daughters of Proetus were as terrified as any cow would be when threatened by men. In the ensuing chase, Proetus's eldest daughter died of exhaustion and the malnourishment from which she already suffered. Fortunately, the other two were captured just in time.

The soothsayer listened to the mooing of the girls, and his fears were confirmed. Hera, Queen of Olympus, had cursed the girls.

Melampus had remembered that the city-state of Argos was sacred to Hera. It resided near one of her favorite groves, the same one where Argus of the hundred eyes had guarded the cow-shaped Io several generations before. Argus's very name, some say, had a relation to the name of the city, and Melampus was certain that the bovine behavior of Proetus's daughters had a relation to the punishment of Io as well. Melampus had deduced that someone had offended Hera, and the girls' insanity was the goddess's revenge. After listening to the remaining two cow girls for some time, Melampus realized that the offenders were the girls themselves. They admitted that the night before they started acting like cows, they had mocked the images of Hera that graced the city.

In order to restore Proetus's daughters, Melampus had to divine the best way to appease Hera. He knew that if he freed the girls from their debilitating condition against the will of the goddess, he would suffer a fate worse than the cow girls had. Employing all of his listening and interpreting skills, Melampus consulted the creatures of nature for the solution to his problem.

Melampus concocted an herbal draught for the girls to drink and devised a purification ceremony that would hopefully please Hera. The soothsayer was already aware from the mooing of the girls that they were sorry for what they had done. With their repentance and Melampus's expertise, the girls were fully restored by the end of the day.

King Proetus was very happy to have his daughters returned to him. As for Melampus and his brother, the King actually did keep with his end of the bargain – though he was quite reluctant. Each brother received a third of the kingdom of Argos. With each third, Proetus gave his daughters' hands in marriage to the two men as well. The dual marriage ceremony was a beautiful one – full of praise to Hera, of course – and they all enjoyed many, many years of happiness together.

The final myth in this section, originating from Ovid, brings all of the previously discussed empowerments into play. It offers the explanations or origins of the Libyan Desert, swans, dark skin, and poplar trees. It teaches lessons about reverence and the dangers of pride and envy. The eternal, unresolved conflict of how the world must cope with the impetuosity of youth is also explored. And, the centerpiece of it all is the personification of the sun, a god who carries daylight across the sky in a chariot. Whether that sun god is Helios or Apollo matters very little; the story is told in relatively the same manner. The central character is still Phaëthon, the son of the sun god and an earthly woman. Phaëthon's actions are legendary. Unfortunately, they are also tragic.

PHAËTHON

"I am the child of the sun!" cried the young man called Phaëthon.

Epaphus, the son of Zeus and Io, rolled his eyes at the assertion. "Phaëthon, my friend, I tire of this bickering. I do not want this competitiveness roused every time someone mentions my mother. Please, do away with this jealousy."

"It is not jealousy!" Phaëthon argued. "I merely want the respect that is owed to me. All of our friends show you so much reverence at times, while I am practically ignored. If my father is as divine as yours, why shouldn't I be given the same treatment?"

Epaphus sighed. "Let us end this, please."

"It will end when you and everyone else believes me!"

"Phaëthon, enough!" Epaphus cried out. "In all of the time that we have been friends, all that I've heard about is how Apollo is your father. You return to that subject over and over again, especially when anyone shows me the least amount of kindness. I wonder, if I were not the son of Io, would you ever think to constantly bring up your own heritage?"

Phaëthon said nothing.

"My mother is adored in shrines across the land," Epaphus continued. "That is not my doing and the shrines are not to me, but people who are believers in my mother's connection to the gods do show me more respect than others. I cannot change that, but I can explain it. There is evidence, Phaëthon. There are those who claim to have seen my mother transform from cow to human. She has given advice that transcends ordinary wisdom. Some have even seen her converse with my grandfather, the river god Inachus. Don't you see, Phaëthon? My heritage is proven by evidence.

Yours is not. I want to believe you, my friend. Perhaps I did in the beginning. But now, you have gone on so long about your supposed father without offering proof that no one is willing to give you the benefit of the doubt. Not even me."

Phaëthon lowered his head. What Epaphus had said was correct. He was not getting the respect that he believed he deserved because there was no evidence that he was the true son of Apollo. Phaëthon had only the word of his mother Clymene to assert his parentage to the world, and that, he now found, was not nearly enough. He would need proof.

That evening, the dejected young man steeled himself to confront his mother. He did not wish to dishonor her with accusations of lying, but he could no longer go on living with only the stories she had been telling him since childhood. She would have to give him more.

He went to her while she was dousing a fire.

"Mother, I have been shamed."

Clymene rose to look upon her son. "Who has shamed you, Phaëthon?"

"You have."

"Really? Tell me how. Tell me how a mother who loves her son more than her own life could have shamed him. Tell me, Phaëthon, of the terrible crime that I have committed upon your head that leaves you feeling so wronged."

"You have told me that I am the son of Apollo."

Clymene laughed. "It is true. Do you not take my word?"

"I once did, but no longer. If my father really is a god, then give me proof. Show me that I am the offspring of the sun god."

"May my life end before the flames of this fire are extinguished if you are not the child of Apollo!"

Phaëthon, his eyes filling with tears, somberly shook his head. "No, Mother," he said. "I need more than this. I need proof."

Clymene finished putting out the fire. "What you need, then, I cannot give to you. You must go to your father. If you pay close attention, I will tell you how you may find your way to your father's home, the Palace of the Sun. It lies beyond the borders of our own land. Once you have arrived there, he will know you, and you may speak with him. He will give you whatever you want."

So, Clymene told her son exactly how to proceed across the land of the Ethiopians, and Phaëthon eagerly obeyed her directions. He traveled without haste, stopping only when food and rest became urgent necessities. The closer he got to the abode of the sun, the hotter the land was to walk upon. The heat might have daunted others, but the increasing temperatures only fueled his determination to continue his journey. Nothing could cause Phaëthon to yield. He was close to his father and to the proof he needed to show his friends back home.

After many weeks, he finally arrived and the Palace of the Sun was more fantastic than Phaëthon had ever imagined. It was an incredible structure of blazing towers of bronze and gold. The doors of the palace were of radiant silver and had been engraved by the most skillful of hands with all manner of decorations. Its brightness was blinding, but somehow Phaëthon was able to approach. Certainly, this ability was already a sign that his mother had been telling the truth.

Phaëthon made his way up the palace's great steps then pushed his way through one of the massive silver doors. He blinked his eyes rapidly to adjust to the even brighter glare within the palace hall and made his way forward. Not far off, seated on a golden throne, was the sun god, Apollo. By Apollo's side were Day, Month, and Year, and, nearby, the Hours sat patiently waiting for the launch of the sun god's horses.

Apollo raised a hand toward Phaëthon. "Why have you come here, my son?"

"Am I…am I your…son?" Phaëthon trembled.

Apollo smiled and glowed more brilliantly. "Yes, Phaëthon, Clymene your mother has always spoken the truth. You are my son, and I am proud to say so. Come, Phaëthon, allow me to give you your due. It has been far too long in coming. Ask anything of me, and I swear by the river Styx that it shall be yours."

"I have been hoping to prove my parentage, and I know how I want to do it. Father, I wish to drive the Chariot of the Sun."

Immediately, Day, Month, and Year recoiled at Phaëthon's request. The Hours began whispering nervously among themselves. Apollo gasped.

"Phaëthon, please do not ask this of me. You are mortal, and the task of driving the Chariot of the Sun is virtually impossible even for those who are divine. My own father, the great Zeus, would not even deign to drive the chariot. It is dangerous not just to yourself, but to the earth itself."

"It is what I want, Father."

"And I must give it to you, for the gods of Olympus may not go back on a promise when it is sworn by Styx. But, please, take the wish back, young Phaëthon, for your own safety. I can give you anything else."

Phaëthon was not moved. "I want to drive the chariot."

"Do you think the ride will be easy? Do you believe that my steeds will do the work for you?" Apollo rose from his throne and approached his son. "They are beasts of fire with wills that are equally intense to the capriciousness of the flame. It takes all of my godly strength to direct their path."

"I want to drive the chariot."

"The swirling currents of the heavens are filled with threats, my son. The creatures of the zodiac do not appreciate the presence of the chariot through their skies and will attack you at every opportunity."

"It is still what I want."

Apollo's countenance grew grim. "Is there nothing that I can say that will dissuade you?"

Phaëthon shook his head.

"Then, so be it."

Upon the orders of Apollo, the Hours reluctantly prepared the fiery horses to be hitched to the chariot. Day, Month, and Year observed the proceedings anxiously, never daring to protest aloud. Apollo spent his time preparing Phaëthon, giving him advice and warnings, covering him in divine ointment to protect him from the searing heat, and finally fitting the crown of sunbeams snugly upon his head. Throughout it all, Phaëthon smiled as brightly as any of the rays of sunlight cascading from his crown. Driving the Chariot of the Sun was going to be the greatest moment of his life.

Before Dawn opened the gates of the sky, Apollo made one final plea to Phaëthon. The sun god's golden eyes looked upon his son with love and concern; his words were filled with distress. Apollo begged Phaëthon to reconsider his foolish desire. The young man would not yield. He took the reins of the four horses in his inexperienced mortal hands and bid his father farewell.

When the gates were opened, Phaëthon goaded the horses with the reins, and the fiery steeds leapt out of the palace and into the sky. Blazing through the sky without the strong hands of Apollo to hold them in check, the horses felt free to tear through the heavens in any way they pleased. Not once did Phaëthon ever have control of the creatures, and terror filled his youthful heart as he whirled around dizzyingly above the earth.

The horses galloped on the air and soared ever higher, heating up those parts of the heavens that had before known nothing but icy darkness. The creatures of the zodiac despised the burning intrusion and lashed out at the novice driver of the chariot. The Scorpion attacked the chariot with its poisonous stinger. The Crab snapped its claws close to Phaëthon's head. Phaëthon cringed at the bottom of the chariot, trying to hide, but the Bull charged after him and the Lion began chasing the horses. Apollo's horses plummeted downward as quickly as they could to escape the pursuing denizens of the sky. The new path of the chariot, though, led to a new horror.

The earth was burning.

Now far too close to the land, the Chariot of the Sun began to scorch the very earth it was meant to light, warm, and sustain. Phaëthon did not have the strength to pull the reins to direct the horses back upward and helplessly watched the destruction that was entirely his fault. Mountaintops became infernos, crops withered, rivers began to dry, and trees became engulfed in flames. Libya became a desert, and Phaëthon's own people, the Ethiopians, were scorched to the point that their skin became permanently darkened. The intense heat even provoked Typhos, the beast beneath Mount Aetna, to blast his abysmal fires into the sky higher than ever before. Worst and most frightening of all, for the first time, Olympus was on fire. Apollo's fears were coming to pass. The world was going to be destroyed.

"Save me, Zeus!" cried out Earth. "Forget our differences for all of our sakes! Forget about Cronus! Forget about Typhos! If I perish, we all will!"

On fiery Olympus, Zeus was already preparing to deal with Phaëthon's folly. He had summoned the Cyclopes and had them rush up to Olympus a most powerful thunderbolt. Zeus grabbed the bolt and hurled it with all of his might.

A flash of lightning was the last thing that Phaëthon ever saw.

The chariot shattered into dozens of pieces, and the horses scattered amidst the heavens. Phaëthon's lifeless body landed in a river. The river nymphs, taking pity upon the poor lad, attended to Phaëthon's body once it had cooled. Eventually, the family of the late, misguided youth found the burial site and lamented their loss.

Clymene wept unendingly. Phaëthon's sisters refused to leave the place of his burial and soon became rooted to the spot and were transformed into poplar trees. Phaëthon's cousin Cygnus wailed in such an awful manner that he too became transformed. As he cursed the skies and mourned away, he turned into the first swan, a low-flying bird that prefers the river to the sky. Apollo was the last to visit the gravesite. When he grieved, the earth remained dark for a whole day.

Part 2

Gods and Goddesses

THE VISITATION

Once upon a time there lived an elderly couple, Baucis and Philomen, and they loved each other very much. They had lived nearly all of their lives together and done so happily, but had known much hardship. The couple never had children and they were always poor. They lived in one of the harshest areas of Phrygia, a land that was populated by far too many foolish people. The couple's neighbors seemed the most foolish and rudest of all of Phrygia's inhabitants, and Baucis and Philomen were often targets of their cruelty. Nevertheless, the poor, old couple considered themselves blessed; they had each other and they were devout worshippers of the gods of Olympus. Though their home was a mere shack and their days were lean and humble, Baucis and Philomen were genuinely happy.

One evening, there was a knock on the door of the shack. Neither Baucis nor her husband expected anyone to call upon them, and they feared that one of their neighbors might be up to a prank. Hesitantly, Philomen opened the door. There before his old eyes were two strangers – weary travelers looking for a place to rest. Without reservation, Philomen bade them to enter his humble abode. He quickly took their heavy burdens from them in his frail arms and then placed a bench before the hearth so that the two might stretch out their aching limbs. Baucis fed the flames with leaves and twigs, fanned the fire with her own bony hands, and prepared a pot of hot water so that she might offer her guests a hot meal.

Philomen brought in some vegetables from his little garden while Baucis sliced up the meats that she had been saving for her husband's next few meals. While the food cooked, both Baucis and Philomen improved upon some of the dilapidated furnishings to which the couple had grown so accustomed, chatting merrily with their guests to boost up their tired spirits. Soon, a table was set in a manner that was more comfortable and hospitable than any table found in the finest of banquet halls. Baucis and Philomen welcomed their guests to food and wine that might not have been considered abundant, but were truly most tasty, with portions that were quite satisfying.

During the meal, the couple chatted on some more, making their visitors as cheery as they were well fed. While serving dessert, Philomen noticed the he had never needed to refill the flagon that contained the wine at the table. The flagon seemed to refill itself. Not wanting to alarm the visitors, Philomen kept the observation to himself, believing that perhaps his imagination had gotten the best of him. However, no sooner had he poured out another two cups of wine for his guests then the flagon was once more magically refilled. Baucis had noticed the phenomenon as well, and she looked upon the happening with great awe. The couple immediately fell to their knees in prayerful supplication for surely this was a sign from the gods.

At first, Philomen believed the sign to be a warning. Perhaps he had not been as hospitable to the travelers as he could have been. He and his wife had a goose that they used as a guardian for their little garden. Maybe, Philomen thought, the goose should have been killed and roasted to show the guests the proper respect. Certain that that was the explanation for the miracle, Baucis and Philomen ran out to the garden and set out instantly to capture the goose.

The goose, though, was in no mood to comply. The elderly couple chased after it as fast as their old legs could carry them, but the bird was always faster. When they thought they had it cornered between the two of them, they would either slip in the dirt or trip over one another. One of the visitors found it impossible not to laugh at the sight and chuckled heartily.

The other visitor stepped forward and said to the now-exhausted couple, "Do not kill the goose. The heavens above have not caused the miracle of the wine. We have. We are gods."

Lightning crashed in the distance, and a fierce light filled the sky. The visitors were transformed into the most brilliant beings Baucis and Philomen had ever seen – tall, golden, and radiant. Both were easily recognizable. The one who had been chuckling was Hermes, the boyish god who loved to laugh. The other visitor – the one who had spoken – was none other than Zeus himself.

"We thank you for your kindness, Baucis and Philomen," Zeus said. "My son and I have traveled much through your land to find mortals who are still faithful and follow the laws of hospitality. We went to all of your many neighbors. None showed us compassion, but the two of you gave to us your hearth, your goodness, and a wonderful meal."

"Great Zeus," Baucis muttered meekly, "please forgive the lowliness of the food we presented to your divinity. We…we are poor."

Hermes laughed and patted the goose on the head. "Don't worry! It was great! Definitely a huge improvement over the last dinner we had here with your former king, Tantalus. In fact, you could have served us the goose's feathers and it still would have been better than dinner with your king. Trust me."

The skies rumbled, and Zeus then said, "The wicked people of this village are going to be punished for their inhospitality, but the two of you will be spared."

Water proceeded to bubble up out of the ground all around the shack of Baucis and Philomen. The earth burst open in a torrent, and, before the couple could fully comprehend all that was happening before their awestruck eyes, their neighbors were gone. The water had swallowed them up. What had once been a village was now a lake. Only the little shack remained.

Baucis and Philomen prayed for the souls of their deceased neighbors, though those neighbors had been cruel to them in life. At the sight of such piety, Zeus transformed the shack into a temple of marble and gold.

"Name anything, Baucis and Philomen," said the Great Thunderer, "and it shall be yours."

The couple deliberated on the offer, then Philomen said, "We wish to be your priests and that our home be your shrine, and we wish to serve you the rest of our days."

Baucis added, "And we wish to meet Death at the very same time, for neither of us can imagine life without the other."

Zeus smiled. "It shall be as you ask. Baucis and Philomen, you are humble and faithful even at a moment when you could have asked for a kingdom and it would have been yours. I marvel at your goodness and am humbled like never before. If only all of your fellow mortals could be as good and as kind as you. Perhaps then the world would know far less pain and sorrow."

Zeus's smile broadened and his eyes began to glow. Hermes tipped his head toward the couple, and then patted the goose again. Light blinded the couple for an instant, and when they were able to see again, the gods were gone.

Baucis and Philomen lived for many years after that fateful night. They served in the shrine of Zeus happily and became an example for all of those in Phrygia who might have followed the path of their drowned neighbors. When the time came for the old couple to pass away from their earthly lives, a most wondrous event took place. As they stood before the entrance to the marble and gold shrine, they were transformed into trees. Baucis became an oak tree and Philomen a linden tree. So closely did these trees grow together that it appears as if they sprout from the same trunk. The miracle of the transformation was a lasting testimony to the two people whose lives humbled the very gods themselves. Wreaths are still placed upon those trees in their honor today.

The story of Baucis and Philomen presents the most "religious" version of the gods that one will ever find. Zeus is the benevolent father testing the morality of his children by observing how they treat one another. In the end, the good are rewarded and the wicked are punished, and Baucis and Philomen stand as models of virtue and goodness. Overall, this is a story that is not unlike the parables and folktales of hundreds of other cultures and belief systems. It is a morality tale intended to remind members of the faith of their duties to their gods and to one another. It also serves to remind them of the inescapable consequences of faithlessness. The theme of the visiting god who tests his followers in such a manner is common in almost every religion.

The similarities, though, end there. Because of the vast body of stories that comprise the life histories of the gods and goddesses of classical mythology, Zeus, Hermes, and the rest of the Olympians have been so vividly characterized that the unfathomable qualities that apply to divinities of other cultures simply do not apply to them. In essence, we know them too well. Their personalities are more human than divine. One of the reasons for the development of such characterization has been previously explored – ancient man, not wanting to feel helpless against the natural world, created beings that were like him and to whom he could make appeals. Another reason for the unique way in which the Olympians developed is the very "organic" quality of storytelling. As generations pass on a tale, nuances are added or removed by the retelling. Through the oral tradition, the story and its characters evolve. Finally, the interaction of subcultures within a people causes a naturally occurring revising of plot points and characterization to take place so that discrepancies might be sorted out. For example, if one tribe of Greeks believes that Zeus is married to Hera and another tribe believes that Zeus united with the nymph Metis, the easiest way to remedy the inconsistency is to either have one mate be the wife and the other be the mistress, or create some way to "dispose of" one of the ladies. Poor Metis became the unlucky one to be swallowed by Zeus.

What we are left with, then, is less of a religion and more of a magnificent, symbolic portrait of the mentality of a civilization grasping to comprehend the world and themselves. The gods and goddesses were representative of the people who believed in them; they were what the people aspired to become as well as what the people already were. As fully developed characters, the gods and goddesses were imperfect, but still majestic. They persevered against Titans and Giants, wielded powers of cosmic proportions, and yet still found themselves feeling sad and vulnerable. The gods were like us in so many ways.

Foremost, the gods of Olympus were not the creators of the world in which they lived. Like mortals, they were inhabitants and had to deal with whatever Earth had in store for them. The Olympians, though, were able to master the elements, and thus deserved the worship given to them by their followers. The skies, seas, animals, vegetation, even the rocks obeyed the commands of the mighty gods. Nevertheless, as masters of a world they did not make, the Olympians were often in a struggle for supremacy with the likes of Typhos and the Giants, sometimes even at odds with the very earth itself.

Likewise, the gods all had to be born from the union of two other beings. Zeus and the Olympians were immortal, but not eternal. Each of their lives had a beginning, and, when we consider the way they fought against their adversaries and the crucial fact that they needed regular sustenance from nectar and ambrosia, those immortal lives might very well have had an end, too. Perhaps the Olympians could not have died in the conventional sense, but there was always the threat of unending torment to consider. The harsh reality for the gods was that none had emerged out of the cosmic abyss by their own volition. They had not existed as long as Earth had. In fact, the Olympians were more accurately the second generation of gods on earth. Preceded by the Titans, the offspring of Earth and Heaven, Zeus and the rest of the Olympians had to overthrow their predecessors in order to take control of the world. This uprising was made possible by the assistance of other Titans who were not satisfied with the rule of the Titan Cronus, Zeus's father. Without such aid, Zeus and his brothers and sisters would have remained in the belly of their father for all eternity.

The gods were powerless against Fate. No matter how mighty the creature, being, entity, or god, Fate would always dictate what would happen. The Olympians were victims of predetermination as often as mortals were. A prophetic warning might be evaded, but when Fate had predestined the outcome of an event, there was nothing that anyone could do. Fate was sometimes personified as a mysterious person, but was often more like a cosmic force. The Three Fates were a different power in the universe. They were the trio of women who determined the length of a mortal's lifespan in the shape of a length of thread. Even over these three beings, Zeus had very little power.

The gods, though mighty, were also victims to internal struggles for they were as prone to the emotions as any human being would be. Jealousy, anger, lust, regret, and sadness plagued the most powerful Olympians as often as they plagued the most common Greek citizen. Sometimes an entire myth was predicated on the emotional state of the god or gods involved. Capriciousness, too, could be found in their behavior; the gods would give in to a whim at any moment, leaving the faithful to wonder whether these "omnipotent" beings were unstable or just a bit eccentric. The Olympians were also guilty of being a far from trustworthy family. Time and again, they bickered, backstabbed, and practiced deception on one another on a regular basis. The deceptions were successful almost every time, calling the "omniscience" of these beings severely into question. Furthermore, the gods were equally susceptible to being duped by lesser beings, including minor gods and mortals.

Beyond simple trickery or jests, the husbands invariably cheated on their wives with mortals as well as other goddesses. The wives, especially Hera, were vindictive and vengeful yet never terminated the marriage nor cheated in retaliation. Aphrodite was the only goddess to ever betray her husband, and, ironically, her husband Hephaestus was probably the only faithful husband in all of Olympus.

The gods were all individuals. They had their own spheres of influence, their own hobbies, and they displayed varying attitudes toward mortals. The Olympians learned and grew over time, and they developed into very real people to the ancient civilizations that believed in them.

But, there were others before them...

DAWN OF THE TITANS

At first there was nothing but the yawning Chasm, a void of emptiness out of which Earth suddenly sprang forth, though it is disputed just how this came to be. Earth (also called Mother Earth, Terra, and Gaea) was a marvelous entity, the first truly tangible thing in the cosmos. Soon after Earth emerged, the Chasm spawned Tartarus the infernal abyss and Eros the elemental force of love. The influence of Eros upon Earth caused the first being to desire a mate, so Earth created Heaven (also called Uranus) to spread over her. She then desired to bear other lesser beings, so when the Chasm produced Air, Day, and Night, Earth reshaped her very self, forming land masses, mountains, and seas. Then she produced the many nymphs that would live upon her. The Dryads were nymphs of the trees, the Naiads were nymphs of the water, the Oreads were nymphs of the mountains, and the Okeanids were nymphs of the streams. For a long time, these female spirits were the only inhabitants of Earth, and all was well. Then, Heaven intervened.

Heaven became desirous of Earth, mating with her often. Their union begat a new race, beings different from all of the others that had been created because they were the first that had been truly born. These were magnificent creatures – beautiful, powerful, and supreme. Heaven called his twelve sons and daughters Titans. He enjoyed seeing these godly beings walk upon Earth. However, he did not treat his next set of children, the Cyclopes, in the same way. There were three of these brutes, Thunderer, Lightner, and Whitebolt. Each had a single eye in the center of its forehead. The Cyclopes had the potential to harness thunder and lightning, to master Heaven's own powers. As they were born, Heaven imprisoned them within Tartarus, intending that they should never be set free. Once they were trapped, Heaven did the same to his next set of children born of Earth, the Hekatoncheires. These were three monstrously huge creatures, each with fifty heads and a hundred arms. Heaven certainly did not want things more ugly than the Cyclopes tainting the hills and fields of Earth, so they too were imprisoned. Helpless to do anything but watch, Earth lamented the fate of her brood.

When Heaven slept, Earth beseeched her first children, the Titans, to help her free their siblings. The Titans were unsure what to do. Some, like Rhea, did not want to defy Heaven. Others, like Hyperion, enjoyed being the supreme gods of Earth and did not want to share the world with the Cyclopes and the Hekatoncheires. Only Cronus (also called Saturn) the youngest of the Titans was willing to aid his mother Earth. He promised he would do whatever was necessary to hinder Heaven's power and free the ones in Tartarus. To begin the liberation, Heaven had to first be taught a lesson.

Out of a new element, gray adamant, Earth crafted a mighty weapon. She gave it to Cronus, who eagerly accepted the gift. The weapon was a curved sickle of astonishing sharpness. Cronus held the sickle tightly while lying in wait for his father to come to his mother in the night.

As Heaven approached Earth intending to mate with her again, Cronus emerged from his cover and swung the adamant sickle at his father, severing the genitals of Heaven. Heaven retreated, experiencing pain beyond comprehension. Victorious Cronus flung the genitals as far as his powerful Titan arm could throw them. Drops of Heaven's blood scattered across the body of Earth, and the union of blood and Earth produced the relentless Furies and the brutal Giants. When the genitals finally landed in the ocean, they mixed with the foam of the seas, and this new union would eventually produce an entirely different sort of being.

Meanwhile, the victory of Cronus had shifted the balance of power on the Earth. Wounded Heaven would never again attempt to assert control over the world or any of its inhabitants. Cronus was installed as the first

King of the Titans, for he had shown courage and might befitting of such a title. He took his sister Rhea (also called Ops) for his wife and queen. Cronus intended to rule sternly but wisely, and all of the Titans pledged their loyalty to him. There was, however, one thing that Cronus swore he would never do. He had no intention of releasing the Cyclopes or the Hekatoncheires. The new King did not want these powerful monsters roaming the land and posing a potential threat to his rule, so he reneged on his promise to Earth.

Cronus wanted nothing to interfere with his supremacy. He was an immortal and he wanted to rule forever. Angry Earth told him that his children would rise up against him and usurp his authority just as he had done to his own father, Heaven. Cronus did not want to believe his mother's words. Nevertheless, he would take no chances. Every time Rhea gave birth, Cronus would immediately swallow the child. Though the children were immortal and would still be alive inside of him, they would remain unable to grow while trapped in their father's stomach. They would never be a threat to his reign. Rhea protested, but Cronus could not be stopped. He swallowed each and every one of his six children.

Or did he?

Zeus, King of Olympus, god of thunder; also called Jupiter, Jove, and the Great Thunderer

Cronus had never swallowed his youngest child, Zeus. Upon the suggestion of Earth, Rhea gave Cronus a stone instead of the baby. Cronus never checked what he was devouring, and so little Zeus managed to escape the fate that had befallen his older siblings. Rhea sent the baby to be raised by nymphs on the island of Crete. Zeus flourished and returned one day to the land of the Titans. He rescued his sisters Hera, Demeter, and Hestia and his brothers Poseidon and Hades from the stomach of Cronus, released the Cyclopes and the Hekatoncheires from Tartarus, and together they overthrew Cronus and the Titans in a fierce battle that lasted for years and ravaged Thessaly. The Titans who battled Zeus and his siblings were chained in Tartarus, while other children of the Titans, such as Prometheus, were allowed to live on Earth because they either helped Zeus or had not intervened. Earth was angry that any of her children should be imprisoned, so she mated with Tartarus and created Typhos to be her newest avenger. When Zeus defeated Typhos, her most powerful offspring, Earth realized that there was nothing she could do. She allowed the new generation to reign without her interference. Zeus and the others made their home on Mount Olympus and ruled as gods. Except for one interruption by the attack of the Giants, those spawned from the blood of Heaven's severed genitals, their reign went unopposed.

To all ancient people, there was a supreme, divine Zeus – but not all of them saw Zeus in exactly the same way or with the same wife. As different tribes and subcultures met and mixed, so did the stories of the King of the Gods. Ultimately we are left with an amalgam of beliefs and tales that form the ruler of Olympus that we know today.

What remains as singularly similar among all of the varied tales of Zeus is his use of lightning. This awesome, destructive force of Heaven was harnessed, controlled, and forged into bolts by the Cyclopes. They bestowed the use of lightning to Zeus as a reward for their release from Tartarus. Thus, Zeus became the Great Thunderer and a power unmatched by anything in creation.

As a god to mortals, Zeus was kind to the faithful, but unforgiving to those who transgressed his laws. Often, he would bestow upon certain mortals special gifts because of their loyalty to him. Frequently, Zeus would observe the activities of his people yet avoid any form of interaction. He was quite satisfied with allowing humanity to make its own mistakes. When a person showed ambition, Zeus was pleased. However, when a person showed too much ambition, thunderbolts would fly. Exactly just how much ambition was too much could vary depending upon the situation.

Mortal women held a special place in the heart of their god, especially if they were young, attractive, and not necessarily single. Zeus "fell in love" countless numbers of times with innocent maidens, and he would come to them in various guises in order to seduce them. He was known to make his initial approaches in the shape of a bird or animal, but he might just as easily take the form of a handsome human male, a friend or lover known to the woman, or something more elemental and abstract like a rain of gold. Some of Zeus's mortal lovers were destined to be honored as the mothers of great heroes. Others might only have known the wrath of Zeus's scorned wife, Hera. None, though, were ever made long-term companions of the King of Olympus.

Such pathological infidelity would seem most unbecoming of the mightiest god of all. Most agree that this was probably not a deliberate choice upon the part of the ancient mythmakers. As stories about Zeus merged over time, people had to negotiate around the tricky issue of a philandering All-Father. Fortunately, it was not impossible. As noted previously, the simplest way to deal with discrepancies within Zeus's continuity was to relegate some of the women to the status of mistress.

The Okeanid Metis was one of the most unique characters in Zeus's history. She was considered by many to be his first wife, taken by Zeus during his time on Crete before the war with the Titans. Metis was known for her prudence and was instrumental in preparing the young god to confront his father, the wicked Cronus. Zeus had intended on attacking his father and the rest of the Titans on his own, believing that his anger would be enough. Metis warned him that he would never survive such a foolish mission. She suggested that he gain the aid of allies as powerful as he. It was Metis who devised the plan to release Zeus's siblings from the stomach of their father. She concocted an herbal mixture that she and Zeus were able to get Cronus to swallow. The mixture caused him to vomit up the five children in his stomach as well as the stone he had swallowed in place of Zeus.

Later, Zeus learned from either Earth or Metis herself that, should the Okeanid bear him a son, the boy would be more powerful than Zeus and would subsequently overthrow him just as Cronus had done to Heaven and Zeus had done to Cronus. To avoid this fate, Zeus tricked Metis into changing her shape and, when she was a small enough in size, he swallowed her. Even though she was trapped inside of Zeus, Metis would still bear Zeus a daughter…sort of.

Once Metis was gone, Zeus needed a queen with whom to rule Olympus.

Hera, Queen of the Gods, goddess of marriage; also called Juno

Zeus had chosen his sister Hera to be his wife and queen. She had a stronger character than their other two sisters, Demeter and Hestia, and she seemed most suited for the role. The union eventually would lead Hera to become the goddess of marriage, a patroness of the joining of man and woman in a sacred bond that was intended to last forever, no matter what the man did.

The ancients had to reconcile the many stories of Zeus and his different wives; they did so successfully by having the King of Olympus stray from his fidelity to Hera again and again. This development would appear to weaken the very nature of the goddess of marriage, for how could she be the representative divinity of the bond between husband and wife when her own husband was off shape-changing and having children with every other goddess and mortal woman in creation? Again, the ancients reconciled the inconsistency by highlighting Hera's strong character. Rather than have the Queen of Olympus become a passive, weak-willed woman who allowed her husband and his mistresses to get away with an offense, she attacked and punished all of those who might interfere with the sanctity of her marriage, especially the innocent women whom Zeus seduced, whether they were aware of his identity or had been duped. By avenging the very wrongs done to her, Hera provided a symbolic warning to those husbands on earth who would do the same as Zeus. Hera is, therefore, a true protector of a realistic, not an idealistic, view of marriage. Though she could be quite vengeful, she has been inaccurately characterized as brutally jealous when she is, in fact, loyal to a husband who is constantly unfaithful. For Hera, the marriage itself is of the utmost importance.

It can be easily forgotten that Hera was also a great supporter of the heroes of ancient Greece. Famous individuals such as Jason would not have gotten as far as they had without the beneficent aid of Hera herself. Her intervention on the behalf of men who strove to do what was right revealed another aspect of the goddess that led her to being as important to the Greeks as her sister Demeter. Any who were respectful to Hera or favored by her because of a relation to another who was extremely respectful could expect her blessings – and these were the blessings of not just the most powerful goddess of all, but the deity most able to sway the will of Zeus. Hera could be the greatest ally to a hero or to the common man.

Unfortunately, those whom Hera felt had been disrespectful to her could expect swift, severe, and very fitting punishment. Sometimes the affront was an obvious one, as in the case of the daughters of Proetus who mocked the image of Hera and were cursed into believing that they were cows. In other cases, the offense might not have been intentional nor even that noticeable. It mattered little to the Queen of Olympus. Any offense, great or small, would yield the same harsh penalty for the offender, one way or another. Hera's punishments did not vary in proportion to the wrong.

One of the most notorious offenses to Hera occurred when a young man had to make an impossible decision. Hera's reaction to that decision would inevitably lead to the deaths of thousands.

THE GOLDEN APPLE

"Enough!" roared Zeus. His words were followed by the roll of thunder echoing throughout the halls of Mount Olympus. "If this bickering persists, I will silence the offender forever!"

"Then choose," answered Hera, showing no fear for the rumbling thunder. "I agree that this has gone on long enough, but your hesitation is what prolongs the matter, not our bickering."

"Yes, Father, choose," Athena said. "Use your great wisdom and give us the answer."

"I should think the answer very simple," said Aphrodite as she arched her back suggestively. "Goddesses are a strong lot. I'm sure my competitors will deal well with defeat."

Hera scowled at the goddess of love. "If only your own husband could have the same confidence in you as you have in yourself."

"How dare you!" cried Aphrodite.

Thunder rumbled again. "Silence!" bellowed the King of Olympus. "These childish arguments will cease as of today! The three of you have been competing over the same silly trinket for an eternity, and I can take no more!"

"Then choose already!" demanded Hera.

Zeus shook his head. "No. I'll not spend my immortal life listening to the moaning and groaning of scorned goddesses. I have sent Hermes down to Earth. He is locating someone who I believe will be able to make the choice."

"A wise seer?" asked Athena.

"Umm…not exactly."

Far away from Olympus, Hermes landed upon Mount Ida near Troy where he found a young man tending sheep. The young man was no ordinary shepherd for he wore the garb of royalty upon his person. He was, in fact, Paris, one of the princes of Troy. Paris was in the fields tending to his father's personal flock of sheep. King Priam had given him this task, one that ought to have been well beneath his station, because his son had continually proven himself the fool. Paris was exceedingly handsome, but he was a bumbler and a coward. Priam was certain that unless Paris was kept at a safe distance, he would somehow lead the kingdom of Troy to ruin.

Hermes, in the form of a fellow shepherd, approached young Paris and greeted him warmly. "Hello, Prince Paris! How goes the shepherding today?"

"Very well, sir, if you are a sheep," Paris replied. "As for me, I am prepared to throw myself from the top of the mountain. Boredom is my mistress, and she won't go away. Nothing ever happens out here."

Hermes laughed. "You are in luck, my friend! Something is about to happen. You are about to be visited by three goddesses."

Paris gave Hermes the most quizzical look.

"Really," Hermes said. "You are about to be visited by Hera, Athena, and Aphrodite."

"Come on, sir. Don't tease me. I've seen so few women of late – believe me, I miss them! I'd gladly accept a visit from the homeliest girl from the poorest village. But I won't be teased, so be off!"

Hermes laughed again. "Have you ever heard about the wedding of Peleus?"

"Huh? You wish to tell me a story now?"

"You did say you were bored."

Paris nodded. "That I did! Tell me a story then!"

Hermes sat beside Paris and began. "Peleus, who is now himself a king, was once one of the greatest of persons in all of Greece. He was an athlete of much renown and he was an equally skilled warrior. Peleus had been one of the Argonauts and had proven himself time and again. The gods looked down upon him with much favor.

"As a reward for his faithfulness and his many exploits, Zeus gave to Peleus the hand of Thetis, one of the fifty beautiful Nereid daughters of the ancient sea god Nereus, in marriage. King Peleus and Thetis fell madly in love with one another, and the gods were happy. A fabulous wedding celebration was planned immediately, and all of the gods were invited. Often, mortals invite the gods of Olympus to their tables, but it is a rare occasion when they actually accept. All of Olympus happily assented to attending what promised to be a most joyful event.

"The only one not invited was Eris, the goddess of discord and Ares' closest ally. Truth be told, no one except Ares actually likes Eris. Her sole purpose is troublemaking, and no one wants a troublemaker at a wedding. Still, Eris showed up to the wedding. When the ceremony had already taken place and the guests had sat down to dinner, Eris appeared and rolled a beautiful golden apple toward the other goddesses. She said to them, 'This is for the fairest among you,' and then she disappeared. Naturally, each goddess thought herself the fairest and reached for the dazzling apple. That started a pretty fierce fight.

"After some time, Zeus was able to threaten most of the goddesses back to some sort of composure. However, Hera, Athena, and Aphrodite would not relent. They all wanted the apple because each still believed that she was the fairest. With a bolt or two, Zeus was able to hush the three of them temporarily. However, Eris had succeeded in ruining the festive atmosphere of the wedding and soon the party ended.

"The arguing of the goddesses, though, did not end. In mortal terms, the fight went on for many, many years. The three of them demanded that Zeus make a ruling on who was the fairest among them. He continually refused, eluding them when he could, throwing thunderbolts when he could not. His patience at an end, he finally determined to find someone suitable to make the decision for him. He chose you, Paris."

Paris screwed up his face. "Uh, I don't get your story. Is it a joke?"

"No."

The young man continued to stare blankly at Hermes. "No, really. I don't get it."

Hermes smiled. "You will."

The air around Paris suddenly filled with a blinding light that seemed to come from everywhere at once. The air crackled with little lightning bolts. Paris covered his face and fell to the ground.

When he finally managed to find the courage to open his eyes, Paris was awed. Standing before him were the three most enchanting women he had ever seen. Surely, they were goddesses.

Hermes had abandoned his disguise and presented Paris to the goddesses. "Prince Paris," he said, "because of your own incredibly masculine beauty, Zeus himself has selected you to be the judge in this matter. Here, I hold the golden apple, and I give it to you. Choose the fairest of the goddesses that you see before you. When you have made your decision, give the apple to her."

Paris took the golden apple, but never looked at it; his eyes could not leave the sight of the goddesses before him. He had long dreamed of getting out of the fields and returning to Troy where he might return to the maiden-chasing he so dearly missed. Now, he could not imagine being anywhere else. No woman he had ever seen had ever measured up to these three.

Hera spoke to Paris first. "I see, good mortal, that you toil in the fields. This is no place for a future ruler. If you choose me as the fairest, I will make you the king of all of the lands of Asia."

"Listen to me, Paris," Athena then said. "You have too often been made to feel like a fool. If you choose me, you will be given all of the wisdom that any mortal has ever had. You will be Troy's most respected citizen and ruler."

"If you choose me," Aphrodite said, "I will give you what you really want. I will give you the most beautiful woman in the world as your own. She will always be by your side, and you'll never be bored."

Paris did not need long to deliberate. Rather than consider any genuine criteria for which goddess was the fairest, he only thought about their offers. Since he was not interested in ruling a kingdom and he already thought that he was as smart as he needed to be, Paris tossed the golden apple to Aphrodite. The goddess of love caught the apple and held it before the others.

Hera and Athena were furious. Both immediately left the scene.

Aphrodite soon gave Paris what he wanted – the most beautiful woman in the world. That woman was Helen, wife of King Menelaus of Sparta. King Menelaus was, of course, not happy about this. When he realized that Paris had taken his wife, he called upon all of the kings and chiefs of Greece to join him in avenging this deed. They agreed, and a fleet of a thousand ships was assembled to attack Troy.

This was the beginning of the Trojan War, the instrument of Hera's vengeance.

The war between the Greeks and the Trojans lasted for ten years. Several of the gods became involved one way or another, but it was Hera who prolonged the span of the war in an effort to completely obliterate Paris's homeland, Troy. Hera used violence, cunning, trickery, and outright manipulation to cause events that would incite battles and spur on the Greeks. She did not revel in the deaths, but she did want to see the walled city of Troy in ruins. This was the Queen of Olympus at her most vengeful.

What Paris had done was not simply insult Hera; certainly, she could not be so easily offended by such a buffoon. Paris's choice led to the unjust dissolution of the sacred marriage between Menelaus and Helen, and that is what truly fueled Hera's wrath.

Aphrodite kept her promise to Paris by using her powers to make Helen believe that she really was in love with the young prince. The goddess of love would never have reversed what she had done. Thus, when Menelaus and the others planned to attack, Hera moved events – and some of the other gods – so that the rightful husband would be reunited with his wife. On the side of the Greeks were Hera, Athena, and Poseidon. Fighting for the Trojans were Aphrodite, Ares, Apollo, and Artemis. Zeus attempted to intercede in order to end the war, but Hera did everything she could, including seducing him, to keep him from saving the Trojans. When the war finally ended and Menelaus and Helen were reunited and reconciled, thousands were dead, but Hera had gotten her revenge. Troy was destroyed.

Poseidon, god of the sea; also called Neptune and the Earth-Shaker

After the battle with the Titans had ended in success for the second generation of gods, Zeus and his brothers Poseidon and Hades drew lots to see how they would now divide the world. Zeus won dominion over the skies, Hades became lord of the underworld, and Poseidon, as most know, became ruler of the seas.

The Greeks often identified the sea as being a different entity than other bodies of water such as streams and rivers. Because of that, other minor spirits appear in myths as being the resident deities of those smaller bodies of water. This fact, though, did not diminish the might of Poseidon, a god second only to the mighty Zeus. Poseidon's realm was of vital importance to the Greeks. They were a seafaring people and knew that the vast oceans meant much more to their future and survival than any small well or babbling brook. They also knew that the force of the sea during a terrible storm could wipe out entire communities. The sea was life and death for the Greeks, and that made Poseidon a god to be respected, a god of immense power.

The symbol of that power was the sea god's famed trident. Poseidon was always in possession of this three-pronged spear; presumably, no one else could have had the strength or ability to wield the artifact. It must also be noted that the trident was not simply an accessory to distinguish the god of the seas from his brothers. It had great powers when thrust into the ground by its owner. Either the land would suddenly yield a spring of water or there would be a devastating earthquake. Here again we see how the ancient mythmakers reconciled the duality of the natural world to support life and to utterly obliterate it. In Poseidon's trident we have an instrument of life and death. Of course, that instrument, as the faithful believed, was being wielded by a being with whom one could reason through devotion and sacrifice.

The power to cause earthquakes was what gave Poseidon the title of Earth-Shaker. Rarely, though, does he use that power throughout the many myths in which he appears. Most likely, the connection between earthquakes and the seas developed from the fact that, in such geographic regions, the duration of an earthquake was accompanied by turmoil on the seas.

Besides the gift of fresh water, Poseidon was also responsible for another gift to mankind. The god of the seas was actually the one who introduced horses to man. Apparently, the imaginative minds of the ancients saw in the white foam of the crashing waves the images of galloping horses. It was believed that Poseidon was carried along in a chariot pulled not by fish but by the most beautiful white steeds. Artists have since illustrated this belief in a myriad of ways. Sometimes the horses are massive, proud beasts, unbridled, but obedient. In other works, Poseidon's steeds are hip-pocampi, creatures that appear to be horses in every respect except that their hindquarters have been replaced with a giant fishtail. Nevertheless, Poseidon is credited with the introduction of the land-based version ridden by mortals.

So closely was Poseidon associated with horses that his offspring often took the form of magical steeds. Poseidon was the father of Arion, the winged horse that some myths claim could talk as well as any man. The sea god's more famous offspring was Pegasus, the winged horse that had sprung from the neck of Medusa when the hero Perseus sliced off her infernal head. Prior to being the hideously ugly Gorgon that could turn men to stone with one glance, Medusa had been a beautiful mortal, known for the luxuriousness of her hair. Poseidon became enamored with her, and he and Medusa made their way to one of Athena's temples for a romantic rendezvous. Athena considered the act an offense and she visited upon Medusa a most terrible punishment. Medusa's beautiful hair was replaced by a tangle of dozens of writhing snakes and her features were horribly disfigured. She became even more horrible to look upon than her two sisters, Gorgons who were already monstrous but were immortal, unlike Medusa. Despite the transformation, Medusa was already with child by Poseidon. When Perseus cut off her head, Pegasus emerged. The horse Chrysaor, a lesser-known creature, also emerged.

Not all of Poseidon's children, though, were horses. Poseidon's wife was Amphitrite, one of the Nereids and thus a child of the ocean. The sea god had as many dalliances as his brother Zeus, but Amphitrite was happily resigned to being the loyal wife and did not seek vengeance as Hera did. Amphitrite gave birth to Triton, Poseidon's most well respected son. Triton was a half man half fish amalgam just as the satyrs were half man, half goat. As Poseidon's son, Triton was given an artifact nearly as powerful as his father's trident. Triton wielded a twisted seashell that could be blown like a horn. The shell was often used to herald the arrival of his father, but it could be used to also make the seas obey. If the shell was blown gently, waves became tamed; if the shell was blown fiercely, sea storms would form. Triton's offspring all took his man-fish form and were probably the inspiration for stories about mermaids.

Poseidon was usually content with his place as second-in-command to Zeus. He had a wonderful palace at the bottom of the Aegean Sea off Euboea, and the fish in the oceans and the people on land all worshipped him. However, there were occasions when he was not happy with the way his brother maintained the realms. Once, he and Apollo attempted to usurp control over Zeus when they believed his rule was unfair. For that offense, Zeus sentenced his brother and son to service the needs of King Laomedon for the span of one year. Laomedon instructed the gods to build a great wall around his city in order to render the place invulnerable to attack. That city was Troy. Poseidon resented the task and the way Laomedon treated him. Ironically, when Poseidon next rebelled against Zeus it was to take the side of Hera and assist in the destruction of the Trojan city and its people. The god of the seas was sufficiently avenged.

Hades, god of the Underworld, god of wealth; also called Pluto and Dis

Since the land itself was Earth, the mother entity from which came all life, Zeus, Poseidon, and Hades only needed to be concerned about the leadership of the skies, the waters, and the area below Earth. It was this area that became Hades' domain.

Whether Hades was always grim or he just became that way from being underground all the time is impossible to say. Predisposition aside, he was the perfect candidate for the job of god of the Underworld. Hades was never known to be of great cheer, he was far from affable, and, in fact, he was never even depicted as ever remotely smiling. Content with his lot in eternity, Hades fulfilled his role in the cosmos with pride and satisfaction. As god of the land of the dead, Hades was charged with ensuring that the souls of those who had passed on were given their proper treatment and placement when they entered his domain. If punishment was to be meted out, he was often the one who would come up with the proper poetic justice for the offender. If ever there was a question about a particular soul's residency, he was fair enough to listen to appeals, but strict enough to make sure that the balance between the living and the dead was never upset. Hades was a gloomy individual and rarely ever left his underground palace. During those times when he did ascend to Mount Olympus for a gathering or festival, the other gods were not that unhappy to see him leave.

The title of "god of wealth" was also used with Hades because it was beneath the earth where one could find precious gems and minerals. It was believed that the farther down into the ground one went, the more riches one would find. Thus, Hades' realm had to be the richest realm in the entire world! If it was, Hades never flaunted it. While the outward appearances of his brothers Zeus and Poseidon were regal and grand, Hades was drab and gray and cared nothing for gems. It can be very difficult to remember that Hades is the god of wealth since he was far more concerned with the dead.

However, Hades was not Death itself. That being was an entirely separate entity. There was no reasoning with Death; it would come eventually for all people. It was then necessary to have a presence to believe in whose very existence would validate another kind of "life" after Death had taken the first one. In Hades, the ancients had hope that their souls would be treated fairly when their lives ended. He symbolized the afterlife – the belief that there was more in and beneath the world than the eyes could see. Thus, Death could never really triumph for that long.

The souls of the dead went on quite a journey when they left the body. After Death had separated body from soul, the soul might wander aimlessly for a time, though some said that Death ushered the soul to the mouth of the Underworld. Others believe that it was Hermes who collected lost souls and led them to his uncle's domain. Once at the mouth of the Underworld, the souls were ferried across the river Styx by the boatman Charon – as long as they had the fee. Often, the dead were buried with coins somewhere on their person for such an eventuality. Once Charon brought the souls across Styx, the souls passed through the front gates of the Underworld. Cerberus, Hades' famous pet and one of the offspring of Typhos and Echidna, guarded the gates. Cerberus was a gigantic beast with three snarling dog heads and the tail of a serpent. Souls could pass the pooch with no trouble on the way in, but once inside, Cerberus would never let them out again. It was a guard dog intended to keep people in rather than keep them out. Cerberus never left his post except for the one time when Hercules carried him out to the surface world as his final labor.

Once in the Underworld, souls had to be judged based upon the way they had lived their lives. There were three primary judges – the brothers Minos and Rhadamanthus, sons of Zeus and Europa, men of supreme justice in life, and Aeacus, former king of Aegina, also a son of Zeus. These three determined the fates of most of the souls, but Hades had the power to overrule their verdicts, though he never did. Depending upon the soul's previous life, it could find itself in one of three places. Elysian Fields was the paradise reserved for heroes and valiant, noble souls. The Gardens of Hades would fill with the somber souls of those who had to drink from the river Lethe, the river of forgetfulness, so that they would not eternally miss the lives they had left behind. Finally, the souls of the wicked were confined to Tartarus, the prison abyss of the Titans. There, Hades created particularly fitting punishments for these evil people, and the Furies tormented them with devices of torture.

Hades was satisfied with his life in the Underworld, but he eventually became lonely and wanted a queen. In his desire to secure a mate, he came into conflict with his sister, Demeter.

Demeter, goddess of agriculture; also called Ceres

No goddess was more actively worshipped in the ancient world than Demeter, goddess of agriculture. Hers was the power of nourishment and sustenance. When crops were abundant it was because Demeter was happy. Demeter was the goddess of corn, the goddess of the harvest, and, therefore, the goddess of life. The last thing the people of the ancient world ever wanted was an angry Demeter. So long as she was respected, the kind and gentle life-loving goddess never gave anyone pause to fear.

Hades changed all of that...

DEMETER AND PERSEPHONE

The meadows were green with life, and the flowers and trees were ripe with beauty. The fair land was in bloom everlasting, a sign that Demeter, goddess of the flower and the grain, was at peace with the world. Demeter moved across the fields and gazed with gladness upon the works she had wrought. Flowers flourished, corn matured, and pastures were richly abundant. Mankind would be blessed by Demeter's bounty. They would share in her happiness as they had for so very long.

The only thing that gave Demeter greater happiness than tending to the seeds in the earth was spending time with her daughter, Persephone. Persephone (also called Proserpina) was a beautiful bloom herself, a girl blessed with the disposition of a gentle wind, the delicacy of a stalk of wheat, and the beauty of the most precious red rose. Persephone loved nothing more than to walk through the meadows of the earth and gaze upon the colorful variety of the floral population. She and her nymph friends would spend endless hours searching through copses and groves, trying to find one pretty specimen after another. Only when the Chariot of the Sun had finished its journey would Demeter and Persephone return home to Olympus, rejoining their divine family.

One evening, Demeter returned to Mount Olympus without Persephone. The goddess of the harvest appeared fraught with fear. She rushed over to her sister Hestia, whose place was eternally at the hearth of Olympus, and spoke words of panic.

"Hestia, have you seen Persephone? Has she returned ahead of me?"

"No," Hestia answered. "I have not seen her since she left with you this morning. What has happened?"

"She has disappeared." Demeter's voice was filled with distress. "This afternoon, she became separated from her friends when they were walking through the fields. The nymphs did not see her again. We searched everywhere calling her name, but she did not answer. We could not find her."

Hestia began to share Demeter's worry. There had been rumors that there were Giants out in the world, the last remnants of the first generation of gods. The Olympians knew that one day the Giants would return to avenge the imprisonment of the Titans. Could Persephone's disappearance be the beginning of the Giants' attack?

"Where could she be?"

"I know," came a male voice from across the room.

Demeter spun around. "Apollo! Do you know where Persephone is?"

"Perhaps," replied the sun god. "As I made my way across the sky in my chariot, I saw the ground open up beneath Persephone. She became engulfed in the darkness that not even my own piercing beams ever reach. But I thought I noted something. She did not seem to fall. It appeared that she had been carried down into the depths."

"Carried?" asked Hestia. "By whom?"

"The only one that I can think of," Apollo answered, "is Hades."

In moments, Demeter brought the disappearance of her daughter to the attention of Zeus. Apollo conveyed what he had seen during the afternoon along with his suspicion of Hades. Zeus considered the matter deeply and then dispatched Hermes to visit the Underworld to learn if Hades had indeed played some part in Persephone's mysterious fate. Fleet-footed Hermes left in an instant.

It was not long before the messenger of the gods returned to Mount Olympus.

"What has Hades said?" Demeter asked. "Has he seen Persephone?"

"Yes," Hermes replied. "He has seen her." Hermes' usual jocularity was gone.

"Then if he has seen her, why are you so grave?" Demeter insisted. "What is going on, Hermes?"

The messenger of the gods sat down. "This is difficult to say, Demeter. It seems that Hades was the one who stole Persephone from you. He has taken her to be his queen."

"No!" Demeter shouted. "I will not allow this outrage!"

Zeus began to rumble. "What did he say, Hermes?"

"Hades invokes his sovereign right to take a queen. He says that he has done no offence in this deed. He says that he has asked for nothing in the past and that he has no need to ask for this. As King of the Underworld, he has the power to choose his queen. Persephone belongs to him."

Shocked by the developments, Demeter petitioned Zeus to intervene, but the god of thunder did not feel that he had the right. It was the privilege of the great ones to take a mate. Most of the time, the taking was a seduction, not a kidnapping. Nevertheless, Zeus felt that it would be hypocritical of him to demand that Hades return Persephone. Though he could not agree with Hades' courting methods, Zeus was resigned to accept what had happened.

Demeter, though, would not accept what had happened. She left Olympus angrily, swearing never to return.

From that moment on, Demeter denied mankind her powers. She was angry and depressed and she missed Persephone desperately. She was unable to give life to the seed or the stalk or the bloom. Throughout the world, crops began to wither, seeds refused to sprout, and flowers wilted and died. The goddess renounced her godhood and remained on Earth. She no longer cared to be an Olympian if she and her daughter were to be treated in such an unseemly manner.

The result of Demeter's agony had little effect on the gods, but the earthbound suffered terribly. The land became cold and lifeless as if the ground itself had become its own sort of corpse. Nothing grew. Animals became the first victims, starving from the extreme lack of vegetation. Mankind was soon to follow.

Several of the gods came down to Earth to beg Demeter to return to the duties that only she could perform. None of them were able to move her.

Demeter continued to grieve for her lost daughter, and mortals continued to suffer. Like the animals before them, mankind began to perish. The planet was becoming a lifeless domain, and now Zeus had no choice but to intervene as much as it pained him to do so.

In a short time, Zeus had done his part. On Mount Olympus he gave his decree.

"What Hades has done," Zeus said, "may have been in his right, but it has not been proper. Demeter has suffered a cruelty that none should ever know. The cold, starving world below is suffering even worse. Therefore, I order that Persephone be returned to her mother, thereby correcting the impropriety and enabling Demeter to bring life to the world again. However, Persephone is Queen of the Underworld and she has eaten of the fruit of the Underworld. She must return to Hades for the span of half of a mortal year. In this way, Demeter and Hades may share Persephone equally, six months each."

No one, not even Demeter, could complain about this arrangement. It came to pass then that Persephone would spend six months with her mother every year. During those months, Demeter would attend to her duties as goddess of agriculture. The world would be bountiful with blooms, trees, grass, fruits, and grains. The world would live again.

When Persephone returned to the Underworld, Demeter would become depressed. She would retreat to Earth and pine away for her missing daughter. As her sadness intensified, the world became colder again. Flowers died, trees lost their leaves, and no crops would grow. It would be that way until Persephone returned to her again. Then, life would return.

Even today the cycle continues. The name "seasons" has been given to that cycle.

Through the myth of Persephone, Demeter becomes the symbol of the seasons on earth. Winter, a time of loss in the natural world, is the expression of Demeter's loss and woe. Likewise, spring is the revival of her time with her daughter and the rebirth of nature. Summer and autumn follow perfectly in the natural/emotional pattern. For the reader of mythology, it is easy to see exactly how the symbolism works. It is also easy to acknowledge the brilliance of the ancient mythmakers in this attempt to explain the natural world.

Hestia, goddess of the hearth; also called Vesta

The last of the original six Olympians fathered by Cronus is far from the least, but there are very few instances of Hestia used in mythology. That is appropriate in the case of the goddess of the hearth. Most myths directly involving the gods are expressions of fierce powers, great upheavals, and major changes to the world. Hestia is, herself, a symbol of constancy in that very unstable world.

As the goddess of the hearth, Hestia's duties are simple. She remains on Mount Olympus and she tends to the hearth, the home fire, usually reported to be in the gods' main hall. She never leaves and, thus, never has adventures nor interacts with mortals. Yet, Hestia is the goddess that most ancient people communicated with on a daily basis because, by extension, Hestia was not only the goddess of the hearth, she was the goddess of the home.

In those households that believed in Hestia, prayers of thanksgiving always preceded meals. It is most likely the case that the prayers were not thanking the goddess for the food; Demeter and Poseidon were surely responsible for what was on the plate. The prayers to Hestia thanked the goddess for the stability of the home. It was important even in ancient times to not only have food to eat, but to be able to have a home in which to enjoy the meal. It is possible that Hestia was also shown gratitude for the unified family.

When people set out to settle new territory, the ash or an actual flame from their previous home's hearth was always transported with them on the journey. Again, this was the symbol of Hestia and the symbol of constancy. No matter where they found themselves, believers would light their new hearths with the remains of their previous hearth, thus keeping the continuity of the previous home's harmony alive in their new setting.

Rome had a particular fascination with Hestia and created a ritual out of her stability. The Romans knew Hestia as Vesta, and they created a famous ritualistic cult around her. Vesta's hearth began in the home, but was extended by the Romans to the broader community as a home. Specific areas were granted a public hearth and, to attend to those hearths, virgins were selected as substitutes for Vesta herself. These were the Vestal virgins, honored young women sworn to keep the public hearth burning. It was believed that as long as the public hearth remained alight, peace and prosperity would be bestowed upon the community. If ever a Vestal virgin was negligent in her duty, the penalty was horrible torture. Such punishment was believed to be proportionately fair. The stability of the community rested on the shoulders of these young women, and everyone took the powers of the public hearth and the blessings of Vesta very seriously.

Like the Vestal virgins, Hestia herself remained unmarried at her own request. She wished never to be subject to anything that might cause her to be distracted from her duties.

Aphrodite, goddess of love; also called Cytherea and Venus

When Cronus threw the severed genitals of Heaven away, procreation did not cease. As described above, drops of blood from the genitals mixed with Earth and gave birth to the Furies and the Giants. The genitals themselves landed in the ocean near the island of Cythera. Out of that union sprang forth the goddess of love. Some called her Cytherea because her birth occurred so near the island, but most referred to her as Aphrodite

No other classical goddess has inspired more works of art than Aphrodite. She is the personification of beauty, the epitome of idealized sexuality, and the inspiration for romance. Unlike Hera, Aphrodite was not interested in marriage; she did not see the need for any ceremony where desire was concerned. Aphrodite had the power to bring hearts together, even when one of those hearts was promised to another, as in the case of Helen and Paris. For this goddess, love was all that mattered. As far as Aphrodite was concerned, the other matters of existence were of very little value when compared to the beauty of romance.

The origin of Aphrodite is an especially suitable one. All life came from the seas, and, somehow, ancient mythmakers were instinctively aware of this, though they had no scientific evidence to support the belief. Similarly, Heaven's genitals were like the raw material from which Aphrodite could be formed. From these instruments of cosmic sexuality, the goddess of love emerged full-grown. It was an unusual parentage, but quite perfect for the kind of goddess Aphrodite was.

Not all sources agree on that origin, though. Homer's Iliad claims that Aphrodite is actually the daughter of Zeus and Dione, the offspring of the Titans of the sea. Poets and lovers, though, prefer the former version.

Zeus knew that Aphrodite's beauty was such that it might one day incite a war between the gods who would want her hand in marriage. That was why he decreed that she should be married to Hephaestus, god of fire and the forge. This was a most ironic pairing. Hephaestus was considered ugly and was often depicted as covered with soot from his long hours at the forge. He was lame and physically incompatible to Aphrodite's pure perfection. Even worse, Hephaestus loved to spend his days toiling in his volcano workshop while Aphrodite preferred surrounding herself with the beauty of nature. Aphrodite and Hephaestus were an unsuitable combination, throwing doubt onto Zeus's matchmaking abilities, but the King of Olympus was proactively perceptive in his command. There could have been a war between the gods for her hand, but that eventuality was avoided.

Zeus's stroke of genius, though, did not stop Aphrodite from having a number of affairs and giving birth to several children, none of whom belonged to Hephaestus. The worst of the marital transgressors encouraged by Aphrodite was Hephaestus's own brother Ares, god of war. Ares had wanted Aphrodite from the moment he first saw her. Zeus's decree had forbidden his marriage to her. However, when Aphrodite came to

Ares, drawn to his good looks and masculine demeanor, the god of war had no willpower to resist. Many times, the two met for stolen moments anywhere they could get them. It was an affair that went on for many years. None of the gods figured out what was transpiring between Aphrodite and Ares, but even suspicion would not have been enough to cool the affair. Though many goddesses had turned Ares down because of his cruelty and brutality, Aphrodite was drawn to him even more, making the situation worse while providing a wonderful template for psychotherapists to wonder about in the future.

Hephaestus, a kind and trusting man, seemed not to notice what his wife was on about for some time. Then, one day, it was revealed that he had known all along. When Ares came to Aphrodite's bed, an elaborate array of chains sprang out from underneath, capturing both of the gods in the act and preventing them from escaping. Hephaestus, the brilliant craftsman, had created the trap to do exactly what it had done. Once the trap had been triggered and the naked lovers ensnared, Hephaestus called all of the other gods to see what he had captured. The humiliation that Aphrodite and Ares suffered at the moment ended the affair…at least for a little while.

One of Aphrodite's greatest loves was the mortal Adonis. Several versions of his story exist, all of which bear a similarity to the myth of Persephone, for the time when Aphrodite is separated from Adonis is supposedly the onset of winter, and their reuniting brings back summer. Regardless of the varying reasons for the seasonal changes, the core of the tale remains the same. Adonis is mortal and must inevitably die no matter how much the goddess of love desires him.

Adonis was extraordinarily handsome, and Aphrodite coveted him early in his youth. She spent as much time with him as she could, even neglecting her duties when they were together. One day while Adonis was out hunting, he and his dogs came upon the trail of a savage boar. Ignoring the words of caution Aphrodite had often uttered to her love, Adonis charged forward, never thinking about the consequences of such an encounter. Just when Adonis thought he had the boar cornered, the creature rushed forward and gored him with its tusks. Adonis had been mortally wounded, and there was nothing that Aphrodite could do. He died in her arms. From his blood, the anemone, also called the windflower, sprang to life.

Another figure closely associated with Aphrodite was Eros, known more popularly as Cupid. The original version of Eros was that of an elemental force that had existed since the beginning of time. Eros was that entity which brought people together. Many myths identified Eros as Aphrodite's attendant or companion and not her son. This Eros/attendant aided her in the same way that the famed Cupid/son version did; both provided the force that connected people together romantically when Aphrodite commanded. In many stories, though, Aphrodite herself is capable of this power.

It should also be noted that Aphrodite was not all roses and soft kisses. When the goddess was disrespected or scorned, she was as capable as Hera of meting out punishment. She was fond of turning people into animals. More often, she would send someone else out to do the job for her. Aphrodite was not very good at confrontations, as was evidenced when she attempted to aid Paris and his forces during the Trojan War. Ultimately, the best she could do was to rouse Ares to fight for Troy. What she did do during that terrible conflict, besides inciting it by turning Helen, that was significant was to protect the Trojan Aeneas, who was supposedly her son. With Aphrodite's intervention, Aeneas escaped the massacre of Troy and went on a great voyage to found an even better city.

With Aphrodite's intervention, Aeneas founded Rome.

Athena, goddess of wisdom; also called Pallas Athena, Tritogenia, Minerva, and the Gray-Eyed One

When Zeus had swallowed Metis, he was not aware that the Okeanid was with child. Though Metis was now living somewhere inside of Zeus's body, she still eventually needed to give birth. That birth would be one of the most painful experiences Zeus had ever faced. The prophecy had said that Metis would bear to Zeus children who would be his equal in wisdom. It would seem fitting then that the child that wished to be born out of both Metis and Zeus would make her way through Zeus's head.

Hephaestus, the great craftsman, was called in when the pains in Zeus's head began raging at Lake Tritonis. The King of Olympus had something inside of his head that wanted to come out. Hephaestus performed the "operation" which merely consisted of splitting Zeus's skull open. When this had been done, Athena emerged, full-grown and wearing armor. Her impressive manifestation must have come as quite a shock.

Athena was indeed as wise as her father, perhaps even more so. Quickly, she became Zeus's most sought after counsel, and her advice was never wrong. In recognition of her station as his favorite child, Zeus gave to Athena his mighty aegis, a breastplate that had the power to fill with terror the hearts of enemies on the battlefield. After Perseus had slain the Gorgon Medusa and used her severed head to defeat his foes, the hero gave the head to Athena who had assisted him in his endeavors. Athena attached Medusa's head to the aegis and made the breastplate all the more horrible to behold.

The aegis was an important part of Athena's warrior regalia because she was often a battle goddess, as fierce in war as was her half-brother, Ares. The difference between Athena and Ares was that the goddess engaged in or supported battles only when the action was necessary for the defense of cities filled with innocent people. Ares loved war for the sake of war and reveled in the bloodshed. Because of his cruelty and malice, Athena despised Ares.

Athena's outlook on battle created for her the role of protector, particularly of places that were advanced in civilization. She despised elements of chaos and destruction. She fought mercilessly against injustice, tyranny, and terror. All monsters could consider themselves hated in the flashing gray eyes of Athena, for all monsters were destructive forces and she would do anything to rid the world of them. Thus, Athena gave tremendous support to all heroes who would take a stand against evil. Perseus, Theseus, Jason, Bellerophon, and Hercules all owe Athena a debt of gratitude for rendering to them invaluable service. It is easily argued that, without the assistance of Athena, none of these heroes would have been successful in their adventures.

Athena is often depicted as a tall, beautiful woman adorned in flowing robes. She is armed with a helmet, a shield, and the aegis. Usually, Athena wielded the lightning spear, a powerful weapon capable of repelling any creature, even a god. The owl, a symbol of wisdom, is often her companion, as is Nike, the minor goddess of victory. In her role as the wise, strategic battle goddess, Athena is assigned the name Pallas, the first half of her full name. Pallas is that part of her dual nature that presides over war so that a victorious outcome might lead civilization on to prosperity and productivity. Pallas is the storm-bringer who will ensure the demise of the forces of chaos through brilliant tactics and the force of justice.

During times of peace, Athena's other nature would take precedence. The quieter times demanded a goddess of wisdom that would help leaders to rule with intelligence and prudence. Athena watched over them with great care. She would look out for the betterment of all people, and inspire them to find ways to improve their lives. Athena encouraged arts, crafts, education, and industry. She was said to be particularly talented with spinning and weaving. Her vast wisdom fueled creative powers that were as impressive as her powers on the battlefield.

When attempting to reconcile the duality of Pallas Athena's character, it would seem that she is nothing more than a deified contradiction. She is at once a fierce warrior, wielding lightning and bearing the severed head of a monster on her breast, and a gentle weaver crafting delicate and beautiful works. On the surface, these might seem to be the descriptions of two different individuals – perhaps, a soldier and a seamstress. In Athena, though, the contradiction is resolved when the world she served is examined more closely. In ancient times, the primary objective was survival, but that survival depended not just upon the procurement of food and shelter. Advancements were being made as populations grew. Tribes came together and shared ideas. Civilization was forming, and power bases of physical and intellectual force were coalescing. As the world became more complicated, wisdom was needed to navigate through good times and bad. Peacetime stagnation could cause a civilization to decelerate and decay. Wartime foolishness had even worse consequences. Therefore, no matter the disposition of the times, survival required progress, progress required productivity, and productivity required wisdom and intelligence. Pallas Athena was wisdom personified. She was the goddess to lead civilization through every stage of its development.

As a being so devoted to intellectual pursuits, Athena remained a virgin goddess much like Artemis. She scorned any god's attempt to court her. In this resolve, Athena held to the highest degree the power of the mind. She was not susceptible to irrational emotions or earthly shortcomings as were the other gods. Her wisdom was maintained with perfect clarity at all times. Athena represented the deified personification of the intellect, a fact supported by her emergence from the head of the most Supreme Being, Zeus.

It is written that the famous city of Athens took its name from Athena. She won the right to claim the city for her guardianship in a contest against her uncle, Poseidon.

Both gods had wanted this area of Attica, but only one of them could have it. Zeus had a difficult time choosing between his powerful brother and his favorite child. It was decided then that there should be a contest between the two to determine who would bring more benefits to this new city. Poseidon and Athena were required to mount the Acropolis, a flat, rocky area at the uppermost point of the city, and bestow a gift upon the people. Whichever gift brought more benefits to the citizens would determine the winner. Cecrops, a wise man of the land whom some say was half dragon, acted as judge.

Poseidon struck the rock with his trident and a spring of water appeared where there had been none before. The citizens gasped. This was impressive.

When it was Athena's turn, the goddess pondered for a moment about the area of the city and what would be the most beneficial and productive gift for the citizens to receive. She raised her lightning spear at the Acropolis and then struck a spot near Poseidon's spring. From between the cracks in the rock, an olive tree emerged, the first of its kind. The citizens were in awe; they had never seen anything like it. Athena explained what benefits they could yield from the produce of the olive tree. She told them that cooking, industry, craftsmanship, and trade would all profit from the gift of the tree. The people believed the wise goddess, and Cecrops proclaimed her the winner. Zeus agreed. The city was named in her honor.

The olive tree would become the source of wealth for Athens. The Athenians, under Athena's tutelage, would become renowned for their artistic abilities and strides in education and government. The olive tree would later become a symbol of hope for the citizens. When the Persian fleet attacked Athens, the Athenians were overwhelmed and retreated in their ships. Athena wished to help her people, but Zeus insisted that Fate, for some reason, had already decreed that the city should fall. The Persians landed and, as decided by Fate, destroyed the entire city including the very first olive tree created by Athena on the Acropolis. When the Athenians saw that tree felled, they were devastated. Suddenly, the olive tree grew anew in an instant. The Athenians took it as a sign from Pallas. They engaged the superior fleet of the Persians and defeated them. Athena's strategy had worked. She might not have been allowed to directly assist her people, but she had raised their spirits by bringing the tree back to life. Athens belonged to the Athenians once more.

Ares, god of war; also called Mars

Ares was of little value to the people who worshipped the Olympians. To the Greeks, the originators of much of classical mythology, he was nothing more than the personification of terrible conflict. Later, he became significantly more important to the Romans who knew him as Mars. They viewed him as a magnificent conqueror, the same image they had of themselves. Nevertheless, the Greeks, from whom most of Roman mythology is derived, did not appreciate the pursuit of war, and barely ever mentioned Ares. He was destructive and his powers yielded nothing but pain and despair.

What good was a war god to farmers, fishermen, and philosophers?

Whereas Athena was a protector from aggressors, Ares was the aggressor, or at least the force behind the true aggressors. When two sides went to war, the battle would only end when one group had been completely butchered by the other. There were no rules of engagement in ancient times, no codes of conduct, and certainly no flags of surrender. Truces hardly existed since the usual motive to incite conflict was in the attacker's desire to take something from the defender. War was an exercise in slaughter – mindless, heartless, and merciless.

That description fits what little we ever see of Ares in mythology. Apart from his tryst with Aphrodite, he spends his time with Eris, the goddess of discord, and a retinue of others, including the personifications of Terror and Panic. They roam the land of mortals, eager to engage in battle. If they cannot find a war, Eris tries to stir up trouble. Ares enjoys the bloodshed, especially when he personally causes it.

However, at heart, Ares is a coward. The wounds of others may entertain him, but he cannot bear being wounded himself. In Homer's Iliad, Ares howls with pain and retreats to Olympus when he is wounded on the Trojan battlefield. On the advice of Athena, the warrior Diomedes charged directly at the god of war with a spear. The weapon pierced Ares' stomach and sent the god into such a fit of pain that his screams made the combatants on both sides pause from their fighting. Ares fled back to Olympus to nurse his wound.

The parents of Ares were Zeus and Hera. Neither showed any pride for him. Zeus detested Ares and often gave voice to his hatred. Hera had some love for her son, but she quickly lost patience with him when he engaged in pursuits that led to nothing but death. The only Olympian who received any pleasure from Ares was Aphrodite.

Aphrodite's husband was never too happy about that…

Hephaestus, god of fire and the forge; also called Vulcan and Mulciber

Hephaestus was the brother of Ares, but there was nothing about these two gods that was the same, save their parents. Hephaestus was as kind and gentle as Ares was cruel and bloodthirsty. For Hephaestus, satisfaction was found in creating things, whereas Ares enjoyed destruction. Their character traits were extremely dissimilar, but they did share a common love for the same woman, Aphrodite.

That similarity, though it certainly pained Hephaestus, only served to make Ares look worse in the eyes of the other gods. Most forgave Aphrodite the transgression because passion was her domain. In Hephaestus, the other Olympians saw an innocent victim, a good man who had been unfairly wronged by his brother and his wife. He became more beloved than ever before.

Hephaestus spent his days in his volcano workshop on the island of Lemnos with Thunderer, Lightner, and Whitebolt, the Cyclopes who had helped the Olympians defeat the Titans. Together, they forged magnificent objects for the gods of Olympus, like the dreaded aegis that Zeus eventually gave to Athena. As the god of fire, Hephaestus did not produce the flames; rather, he knew how to control and utilize them to make whatever his imagination could conceive. Whether they were weapons, armaments, furniture, or jewelry, the things that Hephaestus crafted were always masterpieces, each one more marvelous than the last. When Apollo killed the Cyclopes in a fit of rage, Hephaestus proceeded in his work alone.

Physically, Hephaestus was not as attractive as the other gods. His foremost defect was his lameness. Though Hephaestus had a strong upper body, his legs were malformed, causing him to walk poorly and in an irregular fashion. The cause of the defect was attributed to either a deformity at birth or as the result of a violent confrontation with Zeus or Hera. Some say Hephaestus's gait was like that of the flickering flame, a fitting description for the god of fire. To assist him when walking with delicate materials, Hephaestus crafted two handmaidens of gold – artificial life forms who continued to help him after the death of the Cyclopes.

Hephaestus's unappealing exterior seemed to be a source of embarrassment to his mother, Hera. Often, the two would quarrel, and Hera would take her dissatisfaction out on Hephaestus in occasionally violent ways. Hephaestus would anger his father, too. As a good soul, Hephaestus labored to maintain positive relations between all of the Olympians. Once too often, though, he would get between Zeus and Hera when they were bitterly fighting. Hephaestus tended to take the brunt of their aggression. On one occasion, he was forcibly thrown out of Olympus by one of his parents. Some accounts give his fall from on high as the origin of his warped legs.

Nevertheless, Hephaestus was a respectful, obedient son. He never questioned Zeus, no matter the task. Most of the time, Zeus wanted his son to craft objects that would benefit mankind. However, one of Hephaestus's most infamous creations, constructed at the behest of Zeus, would bring to the people of the earth a plague of miseries.

THE GIFT OF ALL

Prometheus was the son of the Titan Iapetus and was endowed with the power of foresight. Prometheus followed his visions wisely and counseled others whenever he could. When the Olympians opposed the Titans, Prometheus's foresight showed him that Zeus would be better suited to rule than Cronus, so he sided with the Olympians and brought his brother Epimetheus with him.

After the battle, Prometheus served as a trusted advisor to Zeus. His foresight could predict the future with great accuracy, and this was a boon to the already wise Zeus. So trusted was Prometheus to the King of Olympus that when Zeus wanted to repopulate the world with new men, he assigned Prometheus the task.

Prometheus used clay from the banks of a river in Arcadia to create the new men. He gave the task of creating animals to his brother. Using his foresight, Prometheus made these new men into the image of the gods. He breathed life into each one himself and, when they stirred into existence, Prometheus loved each one of them.

While Prometheus made men, Epimetheus, cursed with hindsight only, was making beasts of earth without considering the ramifications toward the men his brother was creating. Epimetheus made animals that were faster than men and were equipped with sharp claws and teeth.

When Prometheus saw these creatures roaming the earth, his foresight showed him that if men were not given some defense against the predators, their new race would die. He immediately returned to Olympus to ask Zeus for a favor. Prometheus believed that man needed fire. Fire would provide light and warmth but, more importantly, it would provide the protection man needed against the beasts that would stalk them in the dark of night. Zeus did not even consider the suggestion for a moment. He refused Prometheus's request. At the time, Zeus believed that fire belonged only to the gods.

Prometheus's foresight troubled him terribly that evening. He could envision the demise of the race that he had created. Flesh torn from bone. Limbs devoured. Fear in the blackness of night until the wild creatures struck. Prometheus loved the new people that he had made and he could not allow them to suffer and die. That night, Prometheus stole fire from the gods.

When the first fires began to blossom upon the landscape of Earth, Zeus was furious. Mortals did not have the right to use what belonged to the divine. Soon, though, Zeus noticed that many of the fires lit temples that had been built in honor of the gods. Within the temples, men were burning their own food in sacrifice to the Olympians. This development pleased the Great Thunderer.

One day, Prometheus asked Zeus to visit one of the temples. He claimed that men were not sure what to sacrifice to the gods. He asked Zeus to choose. When Zeus arrived, he saw that an animal had been butchered and separated into two piles. One pile appeared to be the animal's hide and entrails, and the other was a pile topped with fat. Zeus selected the fat, for surely the most delectable meats were beneath it. But, that had not been the case. The good meat had been hidden beneath the hide and entrails. What Zeus had selected was a pile of sinews and bones. The god of thunder had been tricked.

Prometheus's foresight had shown him that man would have wasted away if he continued to burn nourishing food in supplication to the gods. He had devised the ploy to bind the gods into accepting the lesser portions of the animals, while the better parts remained for man. The deceit was a victory for mortals, but Zeus had no intention of allowing Prometheus to go unpunished.

Zeus devised retribution that was cunning and proper; it would strike at the very heart of what Prometheus loved most: mankind. Hephaestus was charged with the task of creating something that would lead men to their own doom, something even more deceiving than the trick of the meat. The item would look wondrous and beautiful and give men many pleasant moments, but it would also bring terrible misery and utter despair. From this creation, men would learn about the pains of mistrust, deception, dishonor, and heartbreak.

Hephaestus created woman. The first one was Pandora. Her name meant "gift of all."

Different versions of the Pandora myth abound. The most famous version makes women less of a calamity upon men than the above version. In that variation, Pandora is given to Epimetheus along with a box. She is told to never open the box. Of course, she does and inadvertently releases all of life's ills upon mankind. She closes the box in time to trap "hope" inside.

Prometheus's punishment is to be chained to the Caucasus Mountain. Every day, an eagle swoops down and devours his liver. Every night his liver grows back again so that the horrible torment can be repeated endlessly.

It is important to note that many versions of the Pandora myth overlook one important detail. From the earliest times, it was written that Hephaestus used his wife Aphrodite as his model for Pandora. Considering how the goddess of love had betrayed Hephaestus with his own brother, it leaves very little doubt as to the rationale behind the fire god's choice for a model. Aphrodite had visited upon sweet and trusting Hephaestus the worst sort of pain. Since he had been instructed to create something to hurt mortal men, Hephaestus naturally chose the suffering that he himself knew all too well.

Thus, the torment of Hephaestus symbolically became the torment of all men.

Hermes, god of thieves and commerce, messenger of the gods; also called Mercury

The lighthearted, boyish god Hermes can be found in more myths than any other god or goddess in classical mythology. That fact is a testimony to what the character symbolized to ancient storytellers.

Full of whimsy and good cheer, Hermes was a lovable rascal. He was clever and quick-witted, had a gift for persuasive speech, and he never seemed to cause trouble on the sort of titanic, mortal-frightening level of his counterparts. He did, however, love a good prank, and from the day he was born to Zeus and Maia, a daughter of one of the Titans, Hermes was a maker of mischief. At the age of one day, he was developed enough in skill and shrewdness to successfully steal Apollo's cattle, making it appear that they had vanished without a trace. The trick had been accomplished with a cleverness that would be Hermes' trademark.

No one had known of the birth of Hermes. Zeus kept Maia hidden away in a cave lest Hera discover his latest affair, so when the little god was born, no one except his mother knew about it. As Hermes peered out at the world beyond his cave, he saw the cattle and instantly devised a plan to make off with them just for the fun of it. The divine infant tied brooms to the back of the legs of all of the cows. He then began herding them into his cave. As the cows walked along, the brooms caused them to brush away their own hoof markings. When Apollo arrived, it seemed that his cows had simply vanished.

A shepherd had witnessed the amazing theft and reported what he had seen to the victimized god. Immediately, Apollo brought the crime to Zeus's attention. The sun god demanded justice. When baby Hermes was brought up to Olympus to face the charges, he was smiling as brightly as he had when he had committed the crime. Hermes admitted the theft and explained that it was just a little joke. As a way to apologize, he presented Apollo with a new musical instrument that he had crafted especially for the sun god out of a tortoise shell. The instrument was called a lyre.

Apollo loved the lyre as soon as his fingers plucked the very first string. Almost immediately, Apollo's anger left him and he and Hermes became the best of friends.

That was the way of Hermes. He was playful, clever, and always thinking ahead. It was no wonder that he became the patron of traders, merchants, and thieves, people who must live by their wits.

Hermes' gear is as famous as he is and is an integral part of his role as messenger of the gods. He carried a curved sword that was remarkably sharp. He only parted with that sword when he allowed mortal heroes to wield it against monsters that would have been invulnerable to ordinary weapons. His magic wand, the Kerykeion, was a winged staff adorned with twisted snakes. His sandals and his hat also featured wings. The latter objects allowed Hermes to move at incredible speeds. His speed made him the perfect messenger.

Stories of the Underworld give Hermes the credit for ushering dead souls to the entrance to their final destination. Most likely, this role developed out of a desire on the part of ancient storytellers to offer comfort to the living. Better to be guided to the Underworld by a smiling, magical jester than the black-cloaked Death.

Like Athena, Hermes was also a great help to heroes. He, too, hated the forces of destruction. He gladly lent his services and even his own equipment to heroes who wanted to rid the land of tyrants and monsters. Those who would make good people unhappy were the enemies of Hermes.

Overall, Hermes was the most popular character in all of mythology because he was the most positive. Whereas other gods would use lightning bolts, enchanted weapons, curses, or horrible plagues to manage their affairs, Hermes relied primarily on a sharp mind, quick wits, and a wonderful sense of humor. Violence was withheld for only the most monstrous of opponents, such as Argus, and goodwill was always the preferred outcome of any conflict, no matter who the opposition was. Hermes, who fulfills the role of the trickster in general mythology, provides a stabilizing force in the Greek and Roman pantheon. He is the god who does not act very godly, he is the fun-loving youth who enjoys being alive, and he is the powerful immortal who just wants to be our friend.

Apollo, god of the sun, light, truth, healing, and music; also called Phoebus, Delian, and Pythian

The little island of Delos was a small and unwanted place. Not attached to any landmass, Delos floated about on the sea, a rejected portion of Earth herself. This unused and unimportant locale seemed to be the perfect place for Leto to take refuge. Leto (also called Latona) was about to give birth to the offspring of Zeus, but the Great Thunderer had abandoned her. After so many years of enduring infidelity, Hera had sworn to unleash a most horrible punishment upon the next woman dallying with her husband, and this threat kept Zeus from doing anything that might give Leto's whereabouts away. Leto's fellow citizens were terrified as well. They feared helping the poor girl lest they be included in Hera's wrath. They even claimed that they had seen a horrible black dragon searching the land in the hope of devouring Leto. Many thought the creature was doing Hera's bidding. It could possibly have been true. The Queen of Olympus had become notorious for her attacks on Zeus's mistresses, especially the pregnant ones, and that left Leto with nowhere to go except the forgotten island of Delos.

The little island gladly accepted Leto and took care of her. Here, Leto gave birth to the twin gods, Apollo and Artemis. Their birth was a wondrous event. Once they were born, Zeus could acknowledge his new children, and the people would revere Leto enough to forbid Hera from making an outward attack. For its part, Delos was rewarded with the highest honor. It would eventually become the location of one of Apollo's greatest temple.

Many scholars have called Apollo the "most Greek" of all the Greek gods. This description is, for the most part, quite accurate. Apollo is the idealized embodiment of what the Greeks believed was the complete man—

handsome, artistic, athletic, wise, caring, and just. Unlike other gods who still retained so many of their unsophisticated traits from the days of early mythmaking, Apollo was a progressive god who seemed to grow along with civilization. He spoke only the truth, healed the sick, took up arms against evil, played sweet, gentle music, and wielded a most deadly silver bow. It is possible that Apollo is as much of an amalgam as Zeus, composed of many different gods merged over time. Still, the god of light has become one of the most well defined deities in all of mythology, a representation of purity, life, and truth.

Though Helios is the god identified as the sun itself, Apollo too is considered the god of the sun just as his twin sister Artemis is considered goddess of the moon. Those who do not make a direct connection between Apollo and the sun do at least acknowledge the significance of light in his sphere of influence. The psychological concepts of light and darkness are essential elements to Apollo's character. Light gives illumination, and illumination brings knowledge. The light of Apollo is, symbolically, both a physical light as well as a mental light. To the loyal believers of the ancient world, Apollo illuminates the way to the truth.

It is within this belief that the roots of Apollo's oracular nature can be found. Followers believed that the deity who was one with light could see and know all things, even the outcome of events. Apollo was then considered the greatest of seers. His power to guide mortals using the way of truth and light was made manifest at the oracle at Delphi near the base of Mount Parnassus. Every year, throngs of people would make their way to Delphi to visit the oracle, a priestess – also called a sibyl – who provided divine answers to any question, in the hope of learning something vital about their present or their future. The oracle at Delphi was considered a genuine and tangible link between men and the gods, a link that had been made possible by the will of Apollo himself.

The oracle at Delphi had been a source of guidance and comfort to the people for many years. One day, a foul black dragon called Python invaded the area near the oracle and threatened the pilgrims who had come to see the sibyl. The people fled from the monster, as did the birds and animals of the land. The priestess who was the current oracle, though, would not leave her post. As evil as the dragon Python was, he was not bold enough to injure the oracle.

After many weeks of terrorizing, Python settled into his new area. He was surprised to find the oracle still sitting on her tripod waiting for pilgrims who certainly would never return. The oracle told Python that the pilgrims would return; his reign of terror would come to an end when the son of Leto came to slay him. Knowing that oracles were never wrong about the future, Python immediately set out to find Leto and kill her before she gave birth. He knew that he could not be slain by someone who had never been born.

The dragon, though, was unsuccessful. He had searched everywhere, only overlooking the most remote or most unappealing places, like Delos. Leto could not be found.

The day came, then, when Apollo, the son of Leto, arrived at Delphi. He was a resplendent sight – a bright, youthful god of light carried on a chariot pulled by magnificent swans. In his hand he carried a silver bow and across his back were stored shining arrows, shafts as sharp as the sun's rays. Python roared defiantly, spewing black venom as he lunged at Apollo. The match, though, did not last very long. Just as the oracle had predicted, Apollo defeated Python. The black dragon's body lay motionless at the foot of Mount Parnassus. Several shafts of light protruded from its lifeless form.

The symbolism of Apollo's reclamation of the oracle at Delphi is easy to interpret. Light had defeated darkness and made the way to the future clear. Apollo had literally and figuratively reopened the path toward enlightenment.

The god of light did not always have to rely upon his silver bow to achieve his ends. He became a skilled musician after Hermes had given him the lyre. It is written that there was no sweeter sound than the melodies created by the lyre's strings plucked by Apollo's divine hands. He played his wondrous music in the great halls of Olympus often, and that made him one of the most beloved among the gods.

Apollo and his father Zeus, however, experienced moments of terrible conflict. On at least two occasions, Zeus had to exile Apollo to Earth to work as a slave to a mortal king. Under Laomedon, Apollo and Poseidon labored long hours to erect the wall around Troy. Under Admetus, Apollo enjoyed beautiful pastures and the friendship of the King. In both cases, Apollo was being penalized for defying the authority of Zeus. In the latter event, Apollo had slain the Cyclopes out of revenge for the deaths of his sons at the hands of Zeus. Phaëthon had been struck by Zeus's lightning when the boy lost control of the Chariot of the Sun, and Asclepius was similarly obliterated when he became too proficient at healing people, robbing Hades of dead souls. Once Apollo had served the duration of his punishment, he was able to return to Olympus and to his dear twin sister whom he missed above all others.

Artemis, goddess of the moon, the hunt, and maidens; also called Diana

Apollo's sister Artemis was the perfect counterpart of her brother. The twins were at once each other's opposite and complement. To understand Apollo was to understand Artemis.

Artemis was the goddess of the moon, confused as often with Selene as Apollo was confused with Helios. As her realm was one of darkness, it might be considered that Artemis was an evil goddess when compared to Apollo's goodness and light. This was not so. The moon, the orb of Artemis, shines through the darkness and mingles with it, offering cool illumination without dispelling the mysteries of the night. Artemis was very much like the moon, cool, subdued, even detached, very much the opposite of her warm and emotionally expressive brother. She was, nevertheless, a protector to the night traveler and to the maiden. Like Athena,

Artemis would belong to no man, god or mortal. Even in the tale of Endymion, she manages to find a way to maintain her virginity.

As the goddess of the hunt, Artemis is often portrayed as a stealthy huntress holding a silver bow like Apollo's. The arrows she used were as gentle and painless as moonbeams. The target experienced no discomfort and fell asleep before finally dying. Her chief companions on the hunt were her faithful hounds and a few loyal nymphs.

Emotionally, Artemis was, again, the opposite of Apollo. Whereas the god of the sun expressed feelings of love and hatred on a poetic scale, Artemis could sometimes be too cool and even pitiless. Unlike most of the Olympians, she asked very little of mortals, but when she believed she had been wronged, her wrath was as dark and as unfeeling as the night itself.

Actaeon learned that the hard way...

ACTAEON

The panicked stag tore through the underbrush, its legs stumbling over a growth of vines.

"Must run," the stag thought. "Dogs. Must run."

Limb after limb smacked at the animal as it blindly charged through the dark woods. The moon was not full, and that made light scarce. Still, the animal's vision was good enough to maneuver. But the panic...the panic made all things impossible.

Like escape.

"Dogs. Not fair."

Close behind the stag came the sound of the pack. The dogs had the stag's scent and would relentlessly pursue. The stag knew that the dogs were hungry. He knew. Their master had deliberately left them without food so that they would be more motivated to chase something, like a deer or a stag.

Like him.

"Must run faster. Dogs. Artemis, please."

The woods had been so familiar to the stag only moments ago, but now everything was different. From this new perspective – from the point of view of the hunted – everything looked strange and wrong. Pretty brooks were now annoying obstacles that caused the hoof to stumble and slow. The shady branches thriving with leaves were like hands slapping a doomed prisoner. Death was behind the stag. Death in the teeth of dogs whose master encouraged savagery. They would capture the stag, he realized.

They had to. They were Actaeon's dogs and they had never lost one yet.

"Not fair. Artemis, please. I'm…"

Actaeon, the hunter who had trained the dogs that now pursued the stag, had been very good at his job. Each day or night when he went out to hunt, he always returned with a prize. His dogs had been the envy of the village, and his skills were virtually unmatched. He had given praise to Artemis for his luck in the hunt, but he was just as likely to give praise to himself.

"Must run. Dogs."

Actaeon and his dogs had gone out this night to track down deer. The hunter had expected the evening to be routine, but Fate had otherwise decreed. This evening, Actaeon was going to encounter a most unique creature in the woods.

Deep in the forest, Actaeon's sharp hearing had caught the sound of trickling water in the distance. This, he thought, was the sound of a deer drinking from a nearby pool or stream. He and his dogs followed the sound stealthily. The hunt was on.

As Actaeon moved noiselessly through the woods, he came upon a clearing. The scent of fresh, clean water filled the air, and the trickling had grown louder. The deer had to be very close. He parted the branches that obstructed his view and peered into the clearing.

Bathing in the pool was a young woman of unearthly radiance and divine beauty. Never before had Actaeon beheld such a feminine wonder. His heart raced and his breathing stopped. He knew that he was not looking upon any ordinary girl. This was a goddess.

He had known that it was improper to stare at a young woman bathing, but he could not remove his eyes from the splendor before him. She was magnificent.

One of Actaeon's dogs had disobeyed his command to stay and had followed him to the clearing. The sound of the dog's movement caused the young woman to look in Actaeon's direction. When she saw the hunter gaping at her, the bather's beautiful face turned pitiless and cold.

"No mortal shall say he has seen the goddess of maidens unclothed!" cried Artemis, and the moon seemed to fall from the sky into Actaeon's eyes.

When the hunter could see again, Artemis was gone. He walked over to the pool she had been bathing in and looked around. Yes, it was like she had never been there. Had he just imagined it? Had this been but a dream? He knelt down to splash his face with cold water.

Actaeon saw his reflection and gasped. The face looking back at him was that of a stag. Artemis had changed him into something that would never be able to speak about what he had seen.

Unfortunately, he had also been turned into something that could not cry out for help. At the edge of the clearing, Actaeon's dogs stared at him and snarled. They had his stag scent, and he knew they would not give up until he had been taken down. The dogs rushed forward. Actaeon fled.

"Must run. Dogs." Actaeon the stag ran as fast as he could. "Not fair. Artemis, please. I'm sorry. Please, forgive me."

The stag darted through the forest, but it knew that the dogs would catch him and kill him. They had to.

The stag had trained them too well.

Dionysus, god of wine; also called Bacchus and Liber

Dionysus was the only god to have a mortal parent. Zeus was his father, and Semele, Princess of Thebes and daughter of Cadmus, was his mother. Semele's fate nearly led to the death of Dionysus before he had ever been born.

After enduring more humiliation than any woman or goddess could stand, Hera was not about to allow a mortal princess to give birth to another of Zeus's divine bastards. When she discovered that Semele was pregnant, the Queen of Olympus came down to the Princess and spoke most deceitful words to her. When the conversation had ended, Semele was convinced that she would be closer than ever to Zeus if she could see him in his true godly form. Of course, Hera knew that no mortal would be able to survive the sight of a god in full radiance, but Semele did not realize that. The next time that Zeus was in her presence, Semele persuaded him to swear by the river Styx that he would grant her a wish. Zeus, of course, complied. When Semele wished to see him in his perfect divine state, Zeus begged her to take back the request and told her that the experience would kill her. Hera, though, had expected Zeus to say that and told Semele that if he did, then that meant he was hiding something. Semele insisted and would not take back the request. Zeus had to keep any promise in which Styx had been invoked. He showed Semele his true form, and she was dead in mere seconds. Semele's unborn child, though, was still barely alive. Zeus took the tiny being and attached it to himself, hiding the child within his own flesh. In that way, the baby could continue to grow and could be born, and Hera would never know about it until it was too late.

Once Dionysus had been "reborn," Hermes carried him off to the valley of Nysa to be tended to by the nymphs who lived in the fertile valley. Dionysus needed time to strengthen and mature before the world found out about his existence, and Zeus gave him the opportunity to do so in a manner similar to the Great Thunderer's own upbringing. It was during his time in Nysa that Dionysus acquired his love of the land and the vine. His affinity for wines grew with each passing day. Eventually, he decided that he would go out into the world to teach mankind how to reap the benefits of the vine. His gift to mortals would be intoxicating.

At first, Dionysus had trouble convincing people that he was, in fact, a god. The pantheon had already been firmly established for many, many years, and, with Dionysus's birth having been so secretive, most did not accept the young man's claim. One or two miraculous events later, skeptics became believers. It did take a while, though, to spread the word, and not everyone was so easily convinced even with the miracles.

One day, as Dionysus was strolling the shoreline, a band of pirates docked in a cove saw the ornately adorned god and figured him for the son of a wealthy family. They approached Dionysus, ignored his pleasant assertions of godhood, and carried him on board their ship. Once there, they set out for sea and began questioning the youth about his home and family. Dionysus continued to allege divine status, and this deeply frustrated the pirates. Angered by his refusal to tell them what they wanted to hear, the pirates attempted to bind Dionysus's hands and feet. Mysteriously, the bindings never held. No matter what they used to keep their captive secured, the material would just unravel or fall apart. Still, the pirates refused to take this as a sign. They threatened Dionysus with death unless he cooperated. Dionysus's reply was hearty laughter. Then, the ship immediate ceased forward motion as if an anchor had been dropped. Impossibly, vines had sprouted out of the sea and coiled around the vessel as if they were the thin, writhing tentacles of some underwater beast. The pirates began to panic. Their captive suddenly disappeared and in his place was a ferocious lion. Screaming pirates began jumping ship in the hope of escaping the jaws of the predator on their deck and the vines creeping all around them. As each pirate entered the water, they suddenly were transformed. By the time it was over, the power of Dionysus had turned the pirates into the first school of dolphins.

Not all stories involving Dionysus end in cute, gentle animals like dolphins. A cult sprang up around the worship of the god of wine, and that cult's activities almost always led to terrible violence.

It is the quality of wine, when ingested, to make people happy. Wine also has the ability to bring people to a state of near madness when too much is consumed. Ancient man was well aware of the consequences of drunkenness, and they incorporated wine's more tragic results into the tapestry of Dionysus's myths through the cult of the Maenads. The Maenads (also called Bacchantes) were women who worshipped Dionysus by going into the wilderness and driving themselves insane with wine. While in the woods, the women would often kill small animals for their feasting by tearing the poor creatures apart while they were still alive. The drinking and the bloody revelry would go on for many hours. It was often the case that, when the Maenads eventually recovered, they could not remember what they had done, but that never served as a deterrent from ever doing it again.

The cult becomes an instrument of godly justice in Euripides' play The Bacchae. In it, Dionysus finally returns to Thebes, the home of his late mother, to complete his wanderings. However, he is not given the welcome that he had expected. Many in Thebes do not believe his claim, no matter what he says. Many women, however, become members of his cult. King Pentheus is the most stubborn in refusing to acknowledge Dionysus's identity and, for this blasphemy, he is punished worse than anyone else. The female members of Pentheus's family, including his mother, come "under the influence" of Dionysus and tear him to pieces as if he were a small woodland animal.

Dionysus is the perfect symbolic personification of wine and its effects. A jolly soul always looking for fun, Dionysus can be the source of liveliness for any festivity. If Dionysus is pushed too far, though, all self-control is lost and the outcome is usually disastrous.

The final myth in this section concerns the character of Orion and features several of the gods in their most representative and traditional roles. Like all myths, there are many versions of Orion's tale. This version includes all of Orion's travels across the Aegean Sea.

ORION THE HUNTER

Orion was a hunter of great renown and even greater stature. As the son of Poseidon, he had been blessed with some of the gifts that the gods passed on to their progeny. Orion was powerful and strong with limbs the size of tree trunks. He moved with grace and had finer features than most other mortals. Being the offspring of Poseidon, Orion had an affinity with the wildness of nature, and the need to be allowed to run free was strong in him. Much like a stallion, Orion would not be tethered in any way, not even to the land. It was that desire to be free to roam that led him one day to summon his father.

Standing on Euboea's calm shores, Orion called out his father's name three times. It did not take long for the hunter to receive a reply. The smooth water's surface began rippling and then the waves intensified, crashing against the coast. Out of the highest wave emerged the heads of four white horses, steeds twice as tall as Orion. The bridled horses flowed through the waters as if they were made of the stuff itself, leaping with ease and landing upon the shore. Behind the horses came the chariot they pulled, their master holding the reins. It was Poseidon the Earth-Shaker, god of the seas. Though Orion had seen his divine father before, the god's emergence was no less breathtaking. Poseidon was broad and muscular, his light blue skin glistening with seawater. In one hand, Poseidon held his mighty trident, the reins being gripped in the other. His countenance was stern yet regal, the crown of coral atop his dark hair glowing elegantly in the midday sun. With a forceful tug on the reins, Poseidon brought the horses to an immediate stop before Orion.

"My son," Poseidon said as he examined Orion, "by the looks of you, I would venture to guess that you are still the fittest hunter in all the land! Make this old sea god proud and tell me that it is so!"

"That it is, my father."

"Splendid! You are a man to be esteemed!" Poseidon gave the reins another tug, and then stepped out of the chariot and onto the beach. "So, what causes you to summon me from my kingdom? You know I do not wish to be on the land if it is not necessary."

"Great Poseidon, I do not call you out of haste. I have thought much upon my plight these past few days, and I cannot deny how I feel. I am a hunter; my spirit is true to that form. I can know no other life, for it is the gift for being your son. But I have found of late that there are few beasts left to challenge me here in this land. My hunting must continue, lest I lose my very purpose for being alive."

Poseidon furrowed his brow. "I know what it means to be true to your nature, Orion, but I do not understand the dilemma you face. If there are too few creatures left for your quarry here in this place, why not travel to another? There are islands on the Aegean alone that would benefit by a visit from a hunter of your proficiency. Sail to any of them, and I will ensure your voyages on my waters will always be safe."

"My thanks, gracious god. I agree that I must seek prey in other places, but I fear that ships are not the answer. My spirit will not allow me the patience to remain still on board those slow moving vessel. I become restless and unnerved; I feel as though I am trapped. This is who I am – Orion the Hunter – I cannot be confined by anything, not the deck of a ship nor the seas themselves."

"What is it you wish, my son?"

"I wish for your mercy and your blessing, great Poseidon. If it so pleases you, give me the power to walk on your water so that I may cross the seas and move from place to place to hunt. Free my hunter's spirit to enable me to continue to honor my divine ancestry."

Poseidon turned his cold, blue eyes away from Orion's pleading face. "This I could grant you, my son, for it is within my power to do so. Once, I might have bestowed the power without hesitancy. Now, I am reluctant to do so. My brethren upon Mount Olympus and I have watched the mortals of the earth change and grow over the countless years. Some of these mortals have been touched by us because they are our children like you or because they are special individuals who deserve the attention of the gods. However, some of these mortals have had aspirations that transgress the respect and obedience that they should show to their benefactors. They attempt the godly, and, for that, the King of Olympus decrees unto them a most terrible punishment. I have seen the wrath of Zeus as it strikes down those who would behave as though they mean to be gods themselves. Nothing remains but ashes. It was so with good Asclepius, the son of the great healer Apollo. His was not evil; he was helping people to be free of illness, age, and then death. This, Zeus thought, was too much power in mortal hands. Zeus's terrible bolts killed Asclepius. I fear that you would share that same fate if my heavenly brother deemed that the ability to walk on water was too godly an attribute for a mortal."

Orion's muscular shoulders sank with disappointment. "Surely, you know that I would never be so arrogant as to liken myself to the gods. Father, I am but a simple hunter who wishes only to continue with the hunt. I give praise to you every day for my life and my gifts. I give praise to Artemis, friend to all hunters, for her continued blessings. I wish only to continue praising both of you with my actions, not just my words."

"Your words ring with much sincerity, Orion. Perhaps we might plead your case to Zeus. If he hears you speak, he might be less likely to judge the ability that I grant to you as harshly as he did the abilities of other great mortals. We might even get him to give you his blessing." Poseidon stepped back into his chariot and motioned to Orion. "Let us go to Mount Olympus."

Orion smiled, placed his club and shield in the sand, and climbed aboard the chariot. Poseidon snapped the reins of his horses twice, and the steeds broke out into a run across the beach. With another snap from their master, the steeds began to take flight, soaring into the clouds as easily as they had moved through the ocean. Orion held fast to the railing of the chariot as it left the earth.

Very soon, the sea god's chariot arrived on Mount Olympus. Orion was staggered by the unimaginable magnificence of the palace of the Olympians. Sophisticated ivory archways connected spires of marble and pearl. Fountains of amber nectar flowed abundantly from beautiful stone statues of nymphs and animals. Clouds silently glided through. Everywhere was purity.

Poseidon took Orion past the hearth of Hestia, where both men paid respects to the goddess, and then into the Great Hall of Olympus. Seated on a throne of gold was the King of Olympus, Zeus. Zeus was draped in golden robes and surrounded by the most heavenly golden light. To Zeus's right was his daughter Athena, the goddess of wisdom and her father's most trusted counselor. On the other side of the Great Thunderer was the carrier of Zeus's thunderbolts, the winged stallion Pegasus, Orion's own kin.

"Welcome home again, Poseidon," said Zeus. "You have been absent from Mount Olympus for far too long."

"Thank you, my brother, but I have much to tend to in the oceans below." Poseidon motioned to Orion. "You do remember my son, Orion, do you not?"

"Of course, I do." Zeus smiled. "He has become a great hunter and makes his father proud. He also finds favor with the goddess of hunters, Artemis. Many times she has spoken of his skills."

Upon hearing the compliment, Orion's cheeks became flushed.

Zeus continued. "It is obvious that you have come to petition me about some matter of importance, Orion. Do not fear. You may speak freely, but wisely."

And so, Orion explained to Zeus and Athena about his situation in the same reverential manner that he had explained it to Poseidon. The gods listened attentively to the young man's plea. Orion recalled what Poseidon had told him about past transgressors, and the hunter insisted that he would not be one of them. He would abide by whatever decision Zeus made. Zeus seemed most interested by the request.

"Much prudence has been shown on your part, good Orion," Zeus said. "Whereas other mortals might have beseeched their parent to give in to their requests, perhaps used sympathy to circumvent the authority of Zeus, you have not ignored your father's warnings. You have come here and shown yourself to be noble and true. I believe that you would not use this ability to anyone's harm. I am inclined to grant you your wish." Zeus turned to Athena. "First, what say you, my daughter?"

The goddess Athena stroked the owl perched on her shoulder and spoke to Orion. "I agree with the judgment of my father, and I believe you, Orion. However, there is a delicate harmony that keeps all things moving at the proper pace in the cosmos. Some creatures have legs, some wings, others fins. If the fish was given legs in order to allow it to access more expedient routes across the land to other parts of the seas, it would need to confront a different set of challenges to its existence on its new path. Creatures on land would then have to cope with hundreds of thousands of migrating schools of fish walking across Earth. The relationships would change. Be aware that this will happen to you. As you change your movement, your pace, so will others when dealing with you. The world will react to you differently, Orion, once you possess this new ability. The delicate harmony will balance itself out, perhaps not always in your favor."

"My daughter speaks as wisely as ever," Zeus said. "Heed her words as do I, Orion. You may have this ability if you wish."

Orion did not hesitate. "I do."

"Then, it shall be yours. Poseidon may grant you the ability to walk on water at his discretion. You need not fear any punishments from me so long as you do not overstep your mortality."

Orion bowed deeply. "Thank you, mighty Zeus."

Soon, Poseidon and Orion returned to the chariot and headed back down to Earth. By the time Orion had been taken back to the place where he had first summoned his father, Poseidon had already conferred to him the power that he desired.

"Continue to make me proud, Orion," the sea god said, beaming. "Enjoy the hunt."

"I will…thanks to you."

Orion remained on the shore until Poseidon and the chariot had disappeared beneath the waves. Once his father had gone, he took up his club and shield and made his way to the water. Though he had just experienced the splendor of Olympus, Orion felt even more amazed by the sight of his feet standing solidly on the seawater. Step by step, Orion walked away from the shoreline, still amazed by his new ability. As he continued moving out into the Aegean, his confidence swelled, but his love for the gods increased as well. The hunter whispered praises to all of the Olympians as he moved onward, his steps more lively than ever in his entire life. When he turned back to see where he had started, he was too far away to make out anything distinctly. Orion was out to sea – and on his feet. Free.

Within two days, Orion came to the island of Chios. He had heard that the lands of Chios were filled with all manner of wild animals. Sleeping was difficult for the citizens of the island; either they were taking turns on all-night guard duty with torches aplenty, or the sounds of the howling, roaring animals would constantly wake them up. Though the people had tried to gain control of the predatory animal population of the island for years, what they lacked was a hunter skilled and brave enough to assist them in creating a safe place to live. When Orion arrived on Chios, he immediately presented himself to King Oenopian.

"My name is Orion," he began. "I am the son of Poseidon and a hunter dedicated to Artemis. With your permission, I wish to hunt on your lands."

The King's eyes went wide with shock. "My permission?" Oenopian laughed maniacally. "How can I give you permission to do something in an area that I don't even control? For my entire reign, we've tried to make all of Chios habitable, but we've never been able to rid ourselves of the beasts that roam the wilds. I'll do anything to be rid of those pests!" King Oenopian grabbed a jug and took a long drink from it. The deep red dribble of wine remained on his lower lip. "Orion, son of whoever, I welcome you to hunt in Chios! In fact, if you can get rid of most of the animals – leave us with a manageable amount – I'll give you my daughter's hand in marriage!"

Princess Aero nearly fell from her seat. "Father!"

"Hush, child!" Oenopian waved off Aero. "So, off you go, hunter! If you'd like to leave the names of your kin with my attendants, you know, just in case you should, umm, get hurt, we'll certainly let them know what's happened to you. Good hunting!"

"My gratitude, King." Orion respectfully bowed, then turned toward Princess Aero. "In a few weeks, you shall be my bride." He bowed again and began to leave the citadel.

Aero rolled her eyes and rested her chin in her hand. Orion was attractive, but she had no interest in marrying a hunter.

"Oh, Orion!" Oenopian called.

Orion halted. "Yes, King Oenopian?"

"One question. None of my people ever saw a ship come to the shores of Chios. How did you get here?"

Orion smiled. "I walked."

For the next several weeks, the King did not see Orion, but he heard much about his exploits. The stories of his tracking and killing of the most ferocious predators were supported by a mind-boggling amount of animal skins and carcasses. This pleased the King to no end. Aero, however, was far from overjoyed.

"Look at how many animals he's killed!" shouted the Princess. "I think he's slaughtered every thing with more than two feet on Chios! Probably snuffed a few pets as well – and I'm going to have to marry him because of your stupid promise!"

The King giggled and sipped a bit of wine.

"What is so funny? Would you mind telling me, please? I'd like to find something humorous about marrying a dirty, smelly hunter."

"My dear," Oenopian cooed, "who said I had to keep any promises? I must admit, this Orion has lasted a lot longer than I expected, but there's still a chance that he'll run out of luck one night. Anyway, if he does manage to survive, I'm sure the great Dionysus will provide me with the divine inspiration we need to get you out of the marriage." Oenopian swallowed the wine that remained in his cup.

"Dionysus, huh? Well, I've seen how he inspires you to pass out and fall down the stairs, so don't be upset if I'm a little less than confident."

"Trust me, Aero."

The Princess growled.

Two weeks later, Orion returned to the King with the pelt of a lion. "This, King Oenopian, is the last of the savage beasts that have plagued your lands. I wanted to bring it to you myself."

"Well done, Orion! Chios owes you a debt of gratitude! My men have confirmed for me that you have indeed cleared all of the land from the animals! Incredible! This calls for a celebration in your honor!"

"A wedding celebration?" Orion asked as he glanced at Aero.

The King stuttered. "Well...I...that is...well, it's a hunter's celebration! No need to mess it up with all that marital mumbo jumbo! You can have the Princess's hand at the next celebration. A man of your skills deserves his own party!"

"You honor me, King Oenopian," Orion said humbly.

The King opened a jug of wine. "My pleasure, Orion."

On the following evening, the celebration for Orion commenced with much merriment and even more wine. The festivities were held outdoors – a first in Chios – and all of the citizens on the island attended. Orion was praised and toasted dozens of times; his cup was never without the sweet nectar of Dionysus. The King was constantly at the hunter's side urging him to drink and sing and dance and drink. Within a few hours, the hunter was almost unable to stand. By the time the celebration had ended, Orion was sleeping the deep sleep of Dionysus.

King Oenopian had imbibed the most wine out of all of the revelers, but he was able to remain awake longer than anyone else. He stumbled into Orion's room and stared at the hunter. He needed to think of some way to stop Orion from marrying Aero. Certain that Dionysus would provide an answer, Oenopian kept on drinking. He first thought about fleeing the island with his daughter. That was not such a bad idea. It was no secret that he had always hated ruling Chios, and he had enough wealth to live well anywhere. If not for the relaxation and forgetfulness that Dionysus brought to him, he probably would have left the place sooner! But how could he and his daughter escape the greatest hunter who ever lived? Not only would Orion be able to track them anywhere they went, he could walk on water – and that was the worst part! You could never escape a man who could walk on water! Nowhere was safe from a hunter who could track you down across the seas with ease. You would always be found.

Unless the hunter could not see you.

Unless the hunter could not see.

Oenopian found one of Orion's skinning knives and removed it from its sheath. If it were not for the spirit of Dionysus that flowed inside of his body, Oenopian would never have been able to conceive of such a dastardly solution, let alone do it. But Dionysus was strong within Oenopian, and the wine had given him courage he would not normally have had. Almost without hesitation, the King raised up the skinning knife above the head of Orion, and then thrust it down quickly into each of the hunter's eyes.

Despite the drunkenness, Orion immediately awoke to the searing pain and darkness that had been plunged into his skull. He screamed in agony; the blood poured down his face.

"Sorry, hunter," Oenopian said, "but I couldn't let you have my daughter. We're leaving Chios, and you'll never be able to find us, no matter how good you are at tracking rabbits and bears." Oenopian dropped the skinning knife to the floor. "I really wish I hadn't needed to do that, but what choice did I have? You can walk on water, Orion, and you could have found us anywhere. Now, you'll never find anything. Goodbye." With that, Oenopian left the blinded Orion to suffer all alone in the room. He and Aero were off the island by morning.

When the people of Chios found Orion the next day, they rushed to his aid. Herbs and salves were used to heal his wounds. Night and day he was tended to until his strength returned. Because he was the son of a god, Orion was able to recover from the terrible injury, but his pierced eyes remained useless. He was still blind. When he was finally able to leave Chios, Orion staggered out to sea on his own.

For many days, Orion wandered aimlessly. He was lost, but that troubled him less than the sadness that filled his soul. He could no longer see and, therefore, he could no longer hunt. His life had been taken away, yet he still lived. Because of this, Orion wanted to do nothing but wander aimlessly. Surely, he could have called upon Poseidon again to ask for the sea god's assistance, but Orion was too ashamed by what had occurred. He had promised to make his father proud of him, but his folly had only led him to disgrace.

After many days, Orion came upon an island that emitted a most peculiar sound, a metallic bashing noise. Curiosity led the blind hunter toward the sound, and he put out his hands to feel his way around. Soon, he was touching what felt like a wall of warm, craggy rock. He followed the wall around for a long time. Orion tried to visualize the shape of the tremendous object, but, without his eyes, it was hopeless.

Then the sound stopped. Orion stopped as well. He could now hear a new sound – the sound of very loud, erratic footsteps. Giant footsteps. Someone was coming.

Orion held his ground. He raised his club and prepared to swing it at the first indication of trouble. Tension gripped the hunter more firmly than he gripped his own club.

"There is no need for weapons on Lemnos, good Orion," said a gentle voice in the distance.

"You know my name?"

"I ought to. I'm your cousin."

Orion dropped the club at the revelation. "My…my cousin?"

"I'm Hephaestus, son of Zeus and Hera. We have met before."

"Yes, I remember."

Hephaestus held Orion's hands. "But I do not remember this affliction to your eyes. What treachery has befallen you?"

"I have been a trusting fool," Orion said, and he told Hephaestus all about walking on water and about Chios.

After hearing about what had happened, Hephaestus brought Orion into his volcano workshop. The god limped along while leading the blind hunter into the heat of the volcano. Once inside, Hephaestus gave Orion a seat and some food.

"I will admit," Hephaestus said, "it's good to have some company in this place. When Apollo killed the Cyclopes, I not only lost my assistants, I lost my friends. I made two mechanical helpers, but it just isn't the same." Hephaestus gave Orion a cup of fresh water. "Here, drink this. I'm afraid it's warm, but it's still very good."

"Thank you."

"Your eyes have been badly injured," Hephaestus continued, "but I think that Apollo might be able to heal you. Though his moods are extreme and his anger as stabbing as sunbeams, healing is most special to him. He had taught his son Asclepius the arts because he was a worthy man. You are certainly worthy of benefiting from those arts. You must go to him."

"But I'm blind. I won't be able to find him."

Hephaestus put his big, calloused hand on Orion's shoulder. "I will help you."

Hephaestus bid Orion to make himself at home in the dingy workshop. For several days thereafter, the god of fire toiled without stopping to eat or rest. Metal clanged, fires sizzled, and the workshop flared with the heat of Hephaestus's work. When the job was done, Hephaestus limped over to Orion and directed the blind man's hand over the surface of a smooth, man-shaped object.

"I have made for you what you do lack," said Hephaestus. "Sight. It is a mechanical person just like my helpers, but with a single difference. I have taken great care to fashion its eye so that it may see the way to the Palace of the Sun. Carry it on your shoulders and it will guide you to Apollo."

Orion would have wept at the generosity of kind Hephaestus, but his eyes were too damaged to allow him to cry. He shook the big hands of his godly cousin, and then put the mechanical man on his shoulders. The machine tapped him toward the north, and Orion's blind travels continued.

For many days, the strange duo traveled across the seas to the Palace of the Sun. This journey was different than the last not only because Orion heeded without question the silent directions of the mechanical person on his shoulders. The hunter had something else now that he had been lacking before he had met Hephaestus on Lemnos. Orion had hope.

The pair arrived at the Palace of the Sun in just ten days. Orion was sure that the place must have been as grand as Olympus, but with his eyes so damaged, he would never have been able to know for sure. The machine guided him to the entranceway of the home of Apollo and left him there. Orion would have to go inside on his own.

Once past the entranceway, Orion began calling out Apollo's name. There was no immediate response, but Orion kept trying and continued to wander blindly through the halls. After some time, the Hours found Orion and guided him to their master.

"Who are you?" Apollo asked.

"I am Orion, son of Poseidon. I seek your healing touch, bright Apollo."

Apollo said nothing at first. His face was serious with thought. "You say your name is Orion? Hmm…Orion. Why is that word so familiar to me, yet the man who bears it is nothing more than a stranger to my eyes? What are you, Orion?"

"A hunter by trade and vocation."

"A hunter?" Apollo's beams grew brighter. "Of course! You are one of my sister's followers. If I am not mistaken, you are one of her favorites."

Orion bowed slightly. "I would be honored to think that such is true."

"It is, man! It is! Artemis tells me that she'd heard you had single-handedly cleared an entire island of savage beasts with just a club. Is that true?"

"Sadly, it is."

"Remarkable! But, what has happened to your eyes?"

Orion told Apollo everything from his assembly with Zeus to his travels with the mechanical person. The god of the sun was most moved.

"This wrong shall be made right with healing and not more wounding. I have learned that vengeance is not the path to the truth. When I slaughtered the Cyclopes to avenge the death of my son Asclepius, I did so blindly, for a man who has his eyes may still be unable to see. If I return your sight to you, Orion, will you give me your word that you will not seek revenge against the King of Chios?"

Orion hesitated. Often in his blind wanderings he had thought about exacting revenge against the man who had so cruelly mistreated him. With his eyesight restored, there would be no place on Earth where Oenopian could hide from the greatest mortal hunter. Orion would have his revenge. But now, Apollo wanted him to dismiss his rage and move past the event. Could Orion do it? Could he forget the pain and injustice?

"I promise not to seek revenge. All I wish to do is to return to the life of the hunter – the only life I know."

Apollo smiled and his eyes glowed. "And so you shall."

Blazing warmth cascaded over Orion's face. His dead eyes began to tingle and move. The warmth became light that Orion could now sense – and then could see! He removed the cloth that had covered the wounds and his eyelids were able to open. Though the light was still dazzlingly bright, Orion could almost make out the silhouette of Apollo on his throne. The clarity did not matter to him; he could see again! In a few moments, the healing rays of Apollo diminished, and Orion could view the world as perfectly as ever. He immediately knelt before the sun god.

"Bright Apollo, thank you!" Orion cried. "I am in your debt, as I am in the debt of all of your kin!"

"Rise, Orion. You are a good man. Take my gift and use it well. Be the great hunter again!"

"I will! I promise!"

The sun god rose from his throne. "Allow me to make a suggestion. You have gained great favor with my sister, Artemis, and that is a feat in itself. Except for a young man from long, long ago named Endymion, no mortal has ever captured her attention as much as you have. Join her in the hunt."

Orion's new eyes were wide with amazement. "Me? Hunt with Artemis?"

"Yes. Go to the isle of Crete. You will find my sister's hunting grounds there. I will send Hermes to her with a message about you. She will expect your arrival and, I am sure, welcome it."

Orion did not know how to thank Apollo for this newest of honors. He bowed many times before leaving the Palace of the Sun to make his way to Crete. As he walked across the Aegean, Orion was overwhelmed with awe at how radically his fortunes had changed.

Once he had arrived on Crete, Orion gave thanks to the gods. Zeus, Poseidon, Athena, Hephaestus, Apollo, and even Hermes had all been a part of his journey – a journey that was going to place him in the company of the patroness of all hunters, Artemis. To her, Orion gave just as much praise. Before his prayers had ended, Artemis was standing by his side.

"Welcome, Orion," Artemis said. "Are you ready for the hunt?"

Orion gaped at the silvery, youthful goddess and her train of dogs and nymphs. He stammered, "It is my honor, goddess," and raised his club to his shoulders.

"Excellent!" Artemis replied. "Let's begin!"

And so, for many years, Orion was blessed to be a companion to the goddess of the hunt herself. Artemis and Orion spent many days in the woods, tracking and trapping all sorts of animals. The fact that Orion had cleared all of Chios meant very little; there were even greater challenges waiting in the wilder parts of Crete. Over time, though, Orion's ability to hunt improved tremendously and began to rival even the abilities of Artemis. If this troubled the goddess, no one could be sure, for she did not express emotions readily. One day, she desired to address the subject with her mortal companion.

"Do you grow bored with the hunt, Orion?" Artemis asked while they sat before a fire.

"It is true that I have mastered much, goddess, though I am certainly not as proficient as you are."

"But do you wish for greater challenges?"

Orion nodded. "Yes. I do."

Artemis smiled, a rare sight indeed. "You shall have a challenge, then. I know of a creature that lives in a faraway land to the east. I will have Hermes fetch it and bring it to Crete."

"What is it?" asked Orion.

"That shall remain a mystery. It is enough to say that you must be wary when approaching this creature. It is as deadly as any that you have faced before. It kills men easily."

"Is it clawed?"

"Yes."

"Does it have tough hide?"

"Its hide is like armor."

Orion laughed. "Excellent! Then bring this beast to me and it shall be vanquished!"

Hermes informed Artemis as soon as he had delivered the creature to Crete. Once there, the goddess gave Orion directions to the area where it had been released. Eagerly, the hunter went out into the wild and tracked his mysterious quarry.

Once in the woods, Orion had trouble picking up any unfamiliar tracks. He was certain that an animal that could kill a man easily would be large enough to leave prints or markings of some sort, but Orion could find none. In fact, he found nothing disturbed in the wilds, and this left him perplexed. Surely, a new animal would cause the other animals to react to it because it was an intruder, but the beasts of Crete seemed not to have noticed the new arrival. What exactly had Artemis gotten Hermes to bring to Crete?

Without warning, Orion's heel began to burn as if on fire. The pain quickly spread through Orion's leg and up into his chest. The hunter gasped and dropped his club. His whole body was wracked with an agony beyond imagination. He fell to the ground, unable to move, speak, or breathe.

The last thing that Orion's eyes saw before his mortal life ended was a small, black creature hiding in the grass. It had claws like a crab, a shiny black body, and an upturned tail dripping with poison. It was the first scorpion that Orion had ever seen. It was also the first creature to defeat him. Acknowledging that defeat in his mind, Orion closed his eyes and died.

Upon Orion's death, the gods on Olympus discussed everything that had befallen the hunter. His had been a life filled with challenges and hardships, but he ever remained a good man and a faithful believer. For the honorable way in which Orion had lived his life, all of the gods agreed that the son of Poseidon deserved a memorial in the heavens. Upon Zeus's decree, stars were reshaped to emulate Orion's form. From that moment on and for all eternity, people could look up to the sky and remember Orion the Hunter.

Part 3

Heroes and Monsters

Dragon's Teeth

"Your sister has been stolen from us, and you do nothing?" King Agenor of Sidon roared at his son Cadmus. "For two days she has been missing! For two days, your brothers have been out searching with their men! And for two days, you talk to people? Where is your heart, Cadmus?"

Cadmus did not meet his father's spiteful glare. "Father, I believe that none but a spirit or a god could have taken Europa from our well-defended home. Though they are noble, my brothers wander aimlessly. After much inquiry, I believe that there is a more direct route – through the gods themselves!"

"Bah! This is nonsense!"

"No, it cannot be! There is an oracle at Delphi that can answer any question. I have been assured of its truth!"

King Agenor shook his head. "I have heard of this oracle, too, but I do not believe it can be of any aid in finding the thieves who have kidnapped Europa."

"If thieves they be! Father, give me my retinue of men and I will go to Delphi and ask the priestess what has become of my sister. Then, my men and I will bring her back to you."

Agenor waved his hand dismissively. "Go! Take your men and waste your time! At least the shame of you will be out of my sight."

"Thank you, Father."

Within hours, Prince Cadmus of Sidon was joined by twenty of the finest armed warriors in the kingdom. All were charged with the task of returning Princess Europa, Agenor's only daughter, to her rightful realm, but the warriors noticed a trembling in the voice of the King as he dispatched them to Cadmus's command. The veterans in the group could recognize when a commander's voice betrayed a lack of confidence, and Agenor was certainly not hiding well his displeasure with his son. Most could easily reject it, though, as they had known Cadmus to be a fine leader, an able fighter, and an impressively intelligent man.

Few were surprised when the group first stopped in Delphi to visit the oracle. This was surely what wise Cadmus hoped would aid them before they committed to a direction for their search, and it was, in the estimation of most of the men, the mark of a good commander to utilize strategy before employing tactics. The men waited patiently while Cadmus went in to see the sibyl alone.

As Cadmus entered, his nostrils filled with the scents of burnt offerings and earthy mist. The priestess was seated on a tripod in the center of the temple. He approached her slowly with his head bowed.

"Priestess…"

"Ask your question…Cadmus."

Cadmus swallowed hard and tried to maintain his focus. He knew he would have to pay very close attention to the cryptic answer the oracle was sure to give. "Where is Europa?"

The priestess inhaled deeply and arched her back. As she exhaled, Cadmus thought he heard her hiss his sister's name.

"Apollo has shown me the truth," the priestess said. "Your sister is now Queen to the white bull that is King to all. She reigns in the land of his youth."

Cadmus nodded. He understood the priestess's words.

"She has never been lost," the priestess added. "You are lost."

"Me?"

The priestess pointed to the young petitioner. "Follow the white cow to your home." With that, she leaned forward, for her answer was done.

Cadmus raced out to tell his men what had happened. Though the priestess's words would have been puzzling to others, they made perfect sense to Cadmus.

Cadmus and his family were descended from the revered Io, one of the chosen of Zeus. The story of Io and her transformation into a white cow had been an important part of their family history; it made them feel very special and very close to the gods. Everyone knew that it would only be a matter of time before new blessings would be bestowed upon the family again. It seemed that Europa had been the receiver of these blessings. According to the oracle, Zeus had taken the form of a white bull and carried off Europa to the island of Crete, the land where the King of Olympus had been raised. The island had never known a ruling body as yet, but now it appeared that it would and Europa would be the first Queen of Crete. Glad would Cadmus be to inform his father Agenor of this great honor. Immediately, he ordered one of his men to return to Sidon with the news. Cadmus also told the messenger to inform the King that he and his men would not be coming home. They would be following their own destiny.

In the distance, there stood a white heifer, the symbol of Io, just as the oracle had predicted. Cadmus told his men that they would follow this heifer wherever it went, though he knew not how long or how far it would be. He knew, though, that this sacred animal would lead them to a place that was to be favored by the gods, a place that was to be their new home. The cow began to walk, and Cadmus followed.

Many days later, the heifer came to rest in the middle of a far away field. Cadmus and his men looked all about the untouched realm and gazed with wondered. The area was the perfect site for a walled city – fertile and defensible.

"This is our land!" Cadmus cried out. "This is the land of the cow – Boeotia! Here, we shall build a magnificent city!"

The men cheered Cadmus's declaration, and they were eager to begin the work.

As Cadmus's planning started, his men settled in to camp. One of them went off to a nearby spring to fetch some water, but he never returned. A second was sent to find the first. The second did not return. A third went off in the same manner. He did not return either. It was obvious that something was terribly wrong. Foul misfortune had befallen his loyal followers, Cadmus knew, so he prepared his men to arms and proceeded to discover what had happened.

At the sight of the spring, all appeared calm. Cadmus had his men split up into two groups to cover the area. They would have to resolve this mystery with success and finality or else there could be no way of ensuring that their city would ever come to fruition.

The contingent that Cadmus led carefully moved through the glen toward the south. There were no signs of the three who had been lost. The land appeared innocent and untouched. Surely, there could be no evil here.

The screams in the distance told them that they were right. The other group had found the evil.

Cadmus and his group raced toward the others, swords drawn. The crossed the glen quickly and ran past the spring totally ready for anything that they should face – but they could never have been prepared for the sight that had awaited them.

Cadmus found his first group of men slaughtered by the black and vile dragon that crawled over their bodies. The monster was the length of fifty men and had a mouth filled with dozens of spearhead-sized teeth…a mouth wide enough to swallow a man whole. The dragon cast its sickly white eyes in their direction and roared at Cadmus and his surviving men. Its mouth dripped thick gobs of blood.

"Attack!" screamed Cadmus, and he led the charge against the monster with his sword drawn forward.

The monster reared back and then thrust its jaws forward, snatching one of the men into its mouth and biting him in half. Before anyone could land a blow to the beast, its claws were sunk deeply into two more men. They were torn open before they could even utter a cry.

The battle proceeded with little change. The dragon killed warrior after warrior, and itself felt little pain. Cadmus and some of the remaining men were able to slash away at the beast while it was killing someone else, but the creature showed no signs of even noticing.

Cadmus, enraged by the butchering of his loyal people, gave in to the most primitive of rages and ignored the serpent's superiority. He attacked its accursed head with all of his might, striking wildly while the creature clawed at his remaining friends. Finally, Cadmus's sword found its mark in the throat of the dragon. Cadmus pushed forward and lanced the dragon with all of his might. The sword made its way through the softer flesh of the dragon's throat and came out the other side. The monster fell dead at his feet.

Sadly, none of Cadmus's men had survived the encounter with the dragon. The Prince was left all alone to begin the task of building a city – something that would be completely impossible.

That evening after Cadmus had given his men a decent burial, he lay in the field where the white heifer had rested and he tended to his wounds. A cool breeze brushed against the back of his neck, and he suddenly realized that he was not alone.

"You fought valiantly today, young Cadmus." The voice was female and unfamiliar.

Cadmus turned to see the image of a beautiful warrior woman with an owl flying nearby her armed head.

"Athena!"

"Your unborn city should not have its greatness devoured by that foul beast that you did rightly slay today."

"But I cannot build a city with only my own two hands!"

"Heed my advice, Cadmus," Athena said. "Pull the dragon's teeth from its awful mouth and sow them as if they were seeds. The harvest will be all the help you need." The goddess vanished after that.

Cadmus obeyed Athena's advice. The next day, he went to the dead monster's jaws and pulled out its teeth with the very sword that had killed it. After digging deep furrows in the ground, he planted the dragon's teeth as if they were seeds.

Almost instantly, there sprung from the ground fully grown and fully armed men, ready for battle. The newborn warriors attacked one another upon sight, swords crashing on shields, clubs bashing on helmets. Cadmus, a natural leader, leapt into the fray and began separating the new men and yelling at others. Eventually, he was able to take command of the group. The fighting ceased and they were ready to follow his orders.

The first order Cadmus gave was to make the men pledge their fidelity to the task of building the great walled city in the center of Boeotia. They all swore that they would not stop working until the task was complete and the city was ready to be populated. In return for their obedience, Cadmus would make them all honored among his new citizens.

The men and Cadmus all kept their word. Boeotia was eventually crowned by the famed city of Thebes.

Cadmus, the legendary founder of Thebes, is one of the earliest examples of the hero in classical mythology. For many mythmakers, Cadmus functioned as a model upon which further heroes were based. Many future heroes, though, owed their creations to several different sources rather than just one, much like the way the lives of the gods were created. Genealogically, Cadmus truly is the first hero, preceding the likes of Perseus and Bellerophon by a few generations. Elements within the structure of his story would become more developed in the stories of other heroes but would still be recognizable no matter how sophisticated the stories became. In fact, most hero myths are very much the same.

There were no female heroes in classical mythology. The closest we can get to a female hero is the great athlete and warrior, Atalanta. Atalanta's exploits during the Calydonian Boar Hunt would seem to place her on equal footing with any male warrior in mythology. Her supposed participation on the quest for the Golden Fleece ought to likewise place her among the legendary champions on the Argo, such as Jason and Hercules. Unfortunately, there is no evidence that Atalanta actually did anything during the quest for the Golden Fleece, thus seriously calling her presence among the Argonauts into doubt, and, even though she was the first to wound the monstrous boar, her role in the Calydonian Boar Hunt was far more consistent with the non-heroic roles of most female characters during the generation of Great Heroes. Women, whether common or as uncommon as Atalanta, performed a crucial function in most of the hero myths of classical mythology, but that function, discussed below, was hardly flattering. The victory, honor, and praise that went to a hero always went to a man.

The hero is an entity unlike any other in the canon of mythology. He is not a commoner relegated to one single cautionary tale or adventure; the hero's story is actually comprised of many smaller stories strung together by recurring characters and a series of challenges. The hero is also not a god. Whereas a god's immortality allows him to appear as the same personality in myths that may be set apart by hundreds of years, the hero is mortal and changes over time. The hero may be representative of a specific region and, therefore, have a home. He will grow old in this region after all of his adventures are done, he will have responsibilities – like a family – in this region, and he might become a leader of this region, perhaps even king. Thus, the hero can be categorized as one who exists in a symbolic state between manhood and godhood. He is one of the ordinary consecrated with the potential to become extraordinary.

To separate him from the common man, the hero is given the blood right that allows him to call one of the gods his parent or ancestor. In classical mythology, this is all but a prerequisite. It must be the hero's very biology that allows him to possess divine potential, the ability to accomplish amazing feats. He must be distinguished from the masses not by force of ego but by right of birth. Much like the passage of power from king to rightful heir by bloodline, a god passes greatness to a hero or at least the potential to be great through the same sort of bloodline. Furthermore, a heavenly ancestry makes the hero a favorite of the gods, and he becomes far more likely to benefit from a timely episode of divine intervention when the need arises. Cadmus is the descendent of Epaphus, the son of Io and Zeus, and that is ancestry enough to grant him an opportunity for greatness as well as a visit from Athena. In classical mythology, it is often the case that heroes are born, not made.

Physical power is also a necessary attribute of the hero. Not all heroes may boast of the strength of Hercules, but all of them must be superior specimens, powerful enough to tackle awesome physical tasks. That raw strength must be further augmented by unflinching courage. Every hero is not only willing to face danger, he is eager for it. Finally, the hero's courage must be supported by convictions. The hero's principles may be based upon the tenets of faith, justice, honor, glory, or redemption, but regardless of their nature, convictions are the building blocks of the hero's motivation.

Part of the hero's career must include the vanquishing of terrible monsters. The universal symbol of heroism is the slain monster. The bigger, meaner, and more grotesque the evil that is destroyed, the better the hero. The creature slain must have already racked up an impressive body count; terrorizing a few kingdoms does not hurt either. Furthermore, the hero must not face the monster reluctantly. Like Cadmus, he must charge the creature with all of the fury and righteousness he can muster. Monsters in mythology are nothing more than symbols of destruction and oppression. For the hero to gain fame and legitimize his status, he must slay the aberrations that plague humanity.

The hero in mythology also served a social purpose. The origins of any myth-culture are rooted in the primitive and the unsophisticated. As a culture began to understand the environment and develop intellectually, the base actions of their past became sources of embarrassment and shame. By believing that a hero of incredible wisdom and power existed in those primitive times, a culture could more easily supplant or suppress the memories, even the oral historical record, of those more unbecoming times. The hero becomes the idealized icon who exists to bring dignity to an era when there was little from which to derive any sort of national pride. The hero restored order, eradicated suffering, and brought hope to life – he helped mold society into what it had become, even though he had never existed. This complex social mentality would sometimes result in the placing of this fictional person into the official historical record of the nation. Some of the heroes in classical mythology were often credited as founders. Cadmus was not only believed to be the fated founder of Thebes, he was also given credit for bringing the alphabet to his people. The hero became a national symbol not representative of what the people were, but representative of what the people wanted to believe they were.

Another unique psychological aspect to the hero myth involves temporal clustering. Storytellers and playwrights deliberately brought the heroes of the same era together, an endeavor that ultimately excited the imagination, contributed to the authenticity of the tales, and roused the hearts of believers. Heroes of the same generation suddenly participated in one another's adventures, though that might never have been the case in the original versions of those adventures. Most likely, hero myths were developed independent of one another, but as the stories were told and retold, there was an intrinsic desire to band some of the heroes together in an effort to consolidate their superhuman powers and fortify the authenticity of the myths themselves. Some heroes made minor guest appearances in another's exploits, while others became brothers-in-arms. It seems that as the stories of heroes were passed along, the tales began to intersect at points of commonality. This was especially true for the Athenian hero Theseus, who appears to have had an encounter or adventure with every other hero of his generation.

As interesting as it may be to team up Theseus with Jason and the Argonauts, temporal clustering without rules of continuity usually leaves behind a mass of contradictions. Ancient mythmakers did not work from a codified set of character timelines, so as the points of commonality were made to intersect, paradoxes of the worst order were created, such as when the evil sorceress Medea tried to kill Theseus as the hero first introduced himself to his father, King Aegeus of Athens. Most sources agree that Theseus was sixteen years old at that time, and Medea was married to

Aegeus. Medea could only have been in Athens and married to Theseus's father after the quest for the Golden Fleece and after the end of her marriage to Jason, a span of at least ten years. Thus, if Theseus was one of the warrior Argonauts who journeyed with Jason on the quest for the Golden Fleece, he could have been no more than six years old during that adventure. Theseus may have been a great hero, but it stretches the limits of plausibility a bit too far to think that he was just as great at the age of six.

The fact that there are no definitive versions of any myths does not help the situation.

Despite the incongruities, the hero myths still fulfilled their functions for the people of the ancient world. These stories were loosely divided into three different generations. The first generation, the Early Heroes, was concerned with the first threats to the burgeoning world of civilization. The second generation, the Great Heroes, was the most popular; they were individuals who symbolized the realization of the potential for greatness in all men – except for a single fatal flaw. The third generation, the War Heroes, included the survivors and victims of the Trojan War, the most awful conflict the ancient world had ever known. Homer's Iliad and Virgil's Aeneid are classical literature's primary sources for the War Heroes and, therefore, have been the subjects of innumerable analyses for centuries. The Early Heroes and Great Heroes, however, have all too often been dismissed as trivial bits of entertainment. Those heroes deserve a closer examination.

The Early Heroes – Perseus and Bellerophon

The myths of Perseus and Bellerophon were rooted in the earlier stories of Acrisios and Proetus, those notoriously hateful brothers who had fought against one another for dominion over the city-state of Argos. The brothers had spent their lifetimes at war with each other. Some myths even claim that they had been twins who had physically fought with one another while still in the womb. Acrisios was always the victor of their battles, but eventually, Proetus would be triumphant. As it had been noted in the myth about Melampus, Proetus was able to take advantage of Acrisios's departure from Argos after an oracle had foretold very troubling things to Acrisios about his future. With Acrisios gone to sulk in his citadel at Larisa, Proetus, supported by militia from his wife's homeland, invaded and secured his sovereignty over Argos.

What had distracted Acrisios so much that he would give up his life-long battle against his brother Proetus? The answer can be found in the tale of one of the greatest heroes in all of mythology…

THE GAZE OF THE GORGON (PART I)

The general of the Argive militia stood before his King and waited for a gesture before delivering his field report. Lately, the King had exhibited a tendency toward quick irritability, and the general certainly would not want to be the target of the King's latest tirade. Though the report would tell of another proud victory, the general felt it best to wait until the King was ready to hear any sort of news.

"Well," muttered King Acrisios as he looked down from his throne at the general, "are you going to give me your report or are you just going to stare at me?"

"Oh, um, sorry, Sire. I come with news from the front. Proetus's men have retreated back to Tiryns, having suffered many casualties by the weapons of your loyal forces."

Acrisios looked blankly at the general, giving no outward indication that he had heard a word of the general's favorable report.

The general did not know what to say next. He had given the entire field report – a succinct account of what every king would have wanted to hear – and yet he received no reaction from Acrisios. Usually, Acrisios loved to laud over his brother's failures. Now, he seemed profoundly distracted. In order to avoid being reprimanded again, the general added, "Uh, so we, um, won."

Acrisios rolled his eyes. "Right. We won. Great. Is that all?"

"Yes, Sire."

"Good. Get out."

The general left the throne room as quickly as was respectfully possible. Whatever was bothering Acrisios seemed to have taken all of the joy out of his life, and the general certainly did not want to be around if the King's disposition worsened.

In truth, King Acrisios's mood would not have gotten worse because he was, in fact, as despondent as any man could be. Considering the nature of the situation that he had been keeping to himself, there was very little in all of Greece capable of cheering him up. Even the news of another one of his brother's botched attempts at an invasion could not mollify Acrisios's anxiety. He was virtually inconsolable.

Unbeknownst to his people, Acrisios had been to the oracle at Delphi to ask about his future, and the sibyl who spoke for bright Apollo himself had given Acrisios a "field report" of her own about his future. It appeared that he, the magnificent King Acrisios of Argos, Lord of Larisa, and Descendant of Danaüs, actually had no future.

Acrisios remembered the conversation with the oracle as if he had just heard her accursed words a moment ago.

"Why have you come, Acrisios?" she had asked without ever opening her eyes.

"I need an answer from the oracle, if it is Apollo's will."

"It is. Ask your question."

"Will I ever have an heir to my throne? It has seemed as though I've endured ten lifetimes trying to have a son and all I have managed to sire is a daughter, Danaë. As the sire to everyone in my kingdom, it is my responsibility to produce a male heir so that my rightful rule continues to bless all of Argos, but I have been unable to do so. I fear that my brother Proetus will use this weakness someday to usurp me. Tell me, priestess, will I ever have a male heir?"

Acrisios remembered the sibyl had inhaled deeply before speaking. She mumbled some prayers, and then answered. "There is only Danaë and her son."

"Her son? Danaë has no son."

"She will," the priestess had said, "and he will be your death."

The oracle had spoken, and Acrisios had been living with those words for the last two weeks.

So, it appeared to Acrisios that after a long life of unceasing confrontations with his brother to keep what was his, there would be no son – no King Acrisios II – to carry on his legacy. Acrisios wondered if all of the fighting had been worth anything after all. Years of battles and bloodshed had been his history and the history of Argos. Now, the oracle had predicted his doom, and the end of his reign and the end of his life seemed to somehow be undeniably interconnected. As Acrisios pondered the circumstance, he could not avoid concluding that everything came back to Danaë. She was not male, and that was his first problem. She was also destined to give birth to his killer, and that was an even worse problem.

Acrisios could have accepted the oracle's predictions, maybe found some way to resign himself to his fate, but he had been molded by a life of conflicts and was a stranger to the path of peace. He could react to the oracle's words in only one way. He would fight.

A few days after his most recent victory over Proetus, Acrisios ordered Danaë to be entombed. She was to spend her days living in a pit in the ground, her only contact with the outside world being the sunlight and air that came through the small openings on the pit's "roof," the lid of the prison. This, to Acrisios, seemed a reasonable solution to his dilemma. Danaë would be given food and drink regularly, and that meant that Acrisios would not be guilty of killing his daughter; therefore, he would not incur the wrath of the Furies who despised and punished such crimes with eternal torment. Furthermore, Danaë, now detached from the rest of humanity, would never be able to have the child that was destined to kill Acrisios. The oracle's prediction would not be able to come true, and that gave Acrisios hope for the future. He would be able to relish his victories over Proetus once more. His mood would improve tremendously – and it did.

Two years passed, and the general stood once more before his liege. King Acrisios met the man with the broadest of smiles.

"How goes the battle, General? Have my brother's pathetic mongrels been returned to him in one piece or several? Give me your report."

"My, um, report. Well, the opposing army does not advance, Sire. Proetus's people seem to be considering retreat again. What I really came to report to you was…well…Sire, it, um, seems that the men heard something near Princess Danaë's, um, home."

Acrisios's spine tensed. "What was it, General? What did they hear?"

"It was crying, Sire. They heard a baby crying."

Acrisios nearly passed out when the general had given him the news. After threatening the general with execution if his report turned out to be a hoax, the King immediately set out to Danaë's prison to hear for himself if the report was true. As soon as he arrived at the site, he could indeed hear the sounds of a baby crying.

Acrisios fell to the ground and placed his face against one of the openings. "Whose child is that with you, my daughter? Tell me!"

"It is my child," Danaë shouted. "My son!"

"No!" cried Acrisios. "It is not possible! No man could fit through these openings to reach you!"

"No man did," Danaë answered. "It was Zeus!"

Acrisios froze.

"Zeus saw my state, saw my loneliness. He pitied me for the injustice you wrought upon my innocent head! He came to me in a rain of gold and embraced me. Now, I have my son Perseus to be my company."

Wailing like a wounded beast, the King lamented the power of Fate. It appeared that the oracle's claims were inevitable truths. Still, Acrisios would not accept what destiny had chosen for him. He righted himself, stood before his men, and regained the composure of the victorious commander he had always been.

"General!" Acrisios roared. "You and your men will remove Danaë and her child from this pit immediately!"

"Yes, Sire!"

"Once you've done that, find a good, strong trunk and lock her and the baby inside of it!"

"A trunk? Yes, Sire!"

"Once the trunk is secure, take it to the top of the cliffs and throw it into the sea!"

The general hesitated. "Sire...?"

"Do not question me! Let it be known that the first among you to raise a doubt about my authority will find his tongue removed from his head! Obey my commands! Danaë and her child must be out to sea within the hour, or you will all be executed!"

The general and his men did not delay. They followed the order, as cruel as it was, and Danaë and her child were soon floating away from Argos and out into the unforgiving watery horizon.

Distance, thought Acrisios. As long as he had distance between himself and Perseus, he would be safe. He could not kill the child for the same reason that he could not kill Danaë, but if the two died while out on the ocean, Zeus would look to Poseidon for the blame. Acrisios would be exonerated. He would be safe.

But if Perseus survived, and the oracle's prediction came to pass, Acrisios would one day die by the child's hand. The King tried not to think about it, he tried to go on with the business of war as he always had, but the worry began to grow, to spread. No matter how he tried to fool himself, Acrisios realized sadly that he would never know contentment again. He could only hope that Perseus did not survive....

King Polydectes of the island of Seriphos was a man not unlike King Acrisios of Argos. He was powerful and cruel and very used to getting what he wanted. He also had a brother for whom he had held great enmity, but Dictys, Poydectes' younger sibling, was not at all a combatant like Proetus. Good-natured Dictys would not strike back at his brother no matter what was done to him. He lived the life of a poor fisherman, alone on the outskirts of the kingdom, and never laid claim to those parts of the kingdom that were rightfully his. To Polydectes, Dictys was a pathetic weakling whose existence was inconsequential. For years he had happily ignored his brother, never expecting that he would ever have any dealings with him again. That was why it had come as such a shock to Polydectes that, when he had dispatched his court to locate the most beautiful woman on Seriphos to be his next bride, he learned that the most splendid and radiant of all women could be found living with Dictys.

Upon hearing the news, Polydectes smirked. "This is a joke, right? I know this is a joke. Smelly little Dictys doesn't even have a wife…at least I don't think he does. If he did, she'd be uglier than the fish he catches."

"I assure you it is true, King Polydectes," said the King's advisor. "They say that many years ago, your brother rescued this most glorious woman from a box that was floating in the sea. She and her son have been with him ever since."

"Her son? She has a son? I can't have another heir. I've already got one. But, if this woman is as beautiful as you say she is, I've go to have her. Is she married to my brother?"

"Your brother is like a father to her. Both remain unmarried."

Polydectes applauded. "Perfect! Just perfect! Except for the part about the son. That's not perfect. How old is the boy?"

"He is a not so much a boy for he does fast approach manhood."

Polydectes considered the situation carefully. He could easily order the death of anyone who stood in the way of what he wanted. He had done so many times. However, he was certain that it would hurt his chances with the mother if he executed her son just before he proposed to her. Therefore, he would have to do away with the young man in a subtler manner. This would call for a very sneaky plan.

The word went out to all of the young men of Seriphos that the King was going to be married again. It was customary for the young men to come to a pre-wedding feast to honor the bride. All were expected to bring lavish gifts. Polydectes was sure that a boy who had been living with impoverished Dictys for his entire life would not be able to afford a proper gift, and that would mean that the King would be able to make a "helpful" suggestion to the giftless guest. Polydectes told his court to make sure that the young man, who he had learned was named Perseus, received an invitation.

On the day of the feast, Perseus arrived without a gift, just as King Polydectes had predicted. The young man was as humble as he was handsome and strong. He approached the King upon entering the feast grounds and he bowed before Polydectes.

"King Polydectes, my name is Perseus. I am a poor fisherman with no gift to give to your bride. I did not wish to dishonor either of you by not attending today, but I am here without a present, and that dishonors me. Ask me to perform any deed, and that shall be my gift to the both of you."

Polydectes smiled. "Well, Perseus, you seem quite a noble boy. For you, nothing but the noblest quest would do! Bring me the head of the Gorgon Medusa! If you do so, your name will be famous throughout Seriphos and all of the nations of the world!"

"I shall do as you request," Perseus replied, though he had no idea how to begin the task. Medusa was more of a legend than a real monster. The only people who had ever seen her had been turned to stone, the side effect of the punishment of Athena. Without eyewitness testimony, it would be virtually impossible for Perseus to find Medusa, but he had already given his word to King Polydectes, so he would never be able to return to Seriphos until his quest was complete.

The scenario that would ultimately propel Perseus to heroism – that is, the issuance of an impossible task – would become a major plot device for many more myths to come. Perseus's story would provide the template for this initiation of conflict, and many other heroes would have to endure the taking up of such a challenge. The giver of the challenge not only expected the hero to fail, but also anticipated that the task would lead to the hero's demise, for that is what the challenger truly desires. Additionally, no matter how focused the task, the hero was sure to be distracted, diverted, misinformed, and maligned along the way before he ever even reached the general area of his destination. The journey would be fraught with plenty of danger.

The mark of a true hero, then, was not simply courage. Perseus and his class needed fortitude, patience, colossal endurance, and an unshakeable faith in their own righteousness.

THE GAZE OF THE GORGON (PART II)

For weeks, Perseus sailed from port to port, asking all manner of people for information about the location of Medusa. Those who did not laugh at him told him tall tales or offered innuendo that always amounted to nothing. After some time, Perseus began to think that Medusa did not even exist, but he could not believe that a king would lie about anything, so he proceeded with the search.

Try as he did to hold on to hope, as the days passed with no sign of a Gorgon, the dread built up inside of the young adventurer. Perseus began to live with the realization that he might never be able to return home.

One evening while walking through a remote and rocky region of Thessaly, Perseus encountered a lonely shepherd who appeared to have misplaced his sheep.

"Excuse me," the shepherd called out. "Did you happen to see any sheep along your way?"

"No," Perseus answered. "Have you lost your flock?"

"Yes. The whole bunch of them."

"I mean no offense, sir, but I don't think you'll find them here. This land is barren and treacherous. Sheep would never come out here."

The shepherd pursed his lips. "Are you trying to tell me that I'm looking in a place that is obviously the wrong place to be looking?"

"I'm afraid so."

The shepherd laughed. "Well, I guess you'd know all about that, wouldn't you, Perseus?"

The young man nearly fell over at the sound of his own name. "How do you know who I am?" he asked, gaping.

"I'm Hermes," said the shepherd as he shed his disguise. "I know all about you. You've been sent on an impossible mission – deliberately, I think. The location of the Gorgons is a piece of information even the gods of Olympus do not possess. The only beings that would know where you could find Medusa are the nymphs of the North, but they live within the realm of the Hyperboreans and are just as impossible to find."

Perseus closed his eyes. "Then, it is hopeless."

"Not at all," came a female voice from behind the young man. Perseus turned around and saw the great armed goddess Athena standing by his side.

"There could be a way," Hermes said.

Athena nodded. "Yes, there is. The Gray Sisters know of the old world of the Hyperboreans. They would be able to tell you how to reach the nymphs of the North. Whether they would be willing to tell you is another matter entirely."

"We can be persuasive, I'm sure," Hermes added with a wink. "I'll take you to them myself. First, we ought to outfit you if you're going to be any sort of hero. Here, you can have my sword." Hermes removed his famous curved sword and handed it to Perseus. "I used this to cut the head off of the monstrous Argus with one stroke. If it can slice through his thick neck, it should work on Medusa easily."

"But you won't be able to approach the Gorgon without the ability to see her, and seeing her means certain death," said Athena. "I give to you my shield. Let its mirror-like surface be your guide, for the powers of Medusa are rendered useless when you view her reflection." Athena gave Perseus her magnificent shield. "Now, you are ready for your quest."

"Thank you, goddess," Perseus said, bowing. "No man can accomplish anything without the blessings of the gods. With these blessings, I will complete what has been until now impossible."

"Impossible because it was meant to be that way," Hermes added. "Take hold of my cloak, fellow son of Zeus. We are off to see the Gray Sisters!"

Perseus held tightly as Hermes stretched out his limbs and took flight. They were headed to the desolate plain adjacent to dreaded Tartarus.

It was not long before the pair entered the sinister domain of the Gray Sisters, three terrible hags who cared little for the world except for what pleasures they could take from the suffering of others. According to legend, the Gray Sisters had always been old hags from birth. Whether this was true or not, the stories all agreed that they had been cruel all of their lives, old or otherwise. The physical trait that left the Gray Sisters vulnerable was their blindness for which they had to share the use of a single eye that they passed between one another periodically. Hermes believed that if Perseus could steal the eye in between passes, he would be in a better position to get the Gray Sisters to cooperate.

Fortunately, the strategy worked. As the Gray Sisters were sharing the eye, Perseus leapt in between them and snatched the magical organ. The hags were shocked that anyone less than a god had found their hideaway. Perseus used that fact to impress upon them the urgency of their situation. He assured them that he would not return their eye to them until they revealed the way to the nymphs of the North. The Gray Sisters were not forthcoming at first, but when Perseus argued that their lack of cooperation would result in the tossing of their eye from the highest mountaintop he could find, they were willing to help. Before accepting their words, Perseus warned them that, if they lied, he could easily return and follow through with his threat. The Gray Sisters were not powerful enough to challenge the bold hero. They told him how to find the beings he sought and they assured him that it was the truth. Perseus returned the eye to the Gray Sisters, and he and Hermes were off again.

Soaring through the faraway lands of the North, where it is said that the ancient Hyperboreans still reign supreme in a land of eternal light, Hermes followed the careful instructions of the Gray Sisters, finally coming to rest in a woodland paradise. Immediately, nymphs of all sorts surrounded Hermes and Perseus. Many of the nymphs recognized Hermes, and they welcomed the pair to their perpetual celebrations.

At the eternal celebration, Perseus recounted all that he had been through since the King had issued his request. Hermes added his own distrust of the situation. The nymphs believed that Perseus would be a great hero, and they approved of his objective. The Gorgons had been a threat to their kind in the days before Medusa had become a vile creature. There had always been three Gorgon sisters. Two were foul, winged women who were evil and immortal. The third was Medusa and she had somehow been spared the Gorgon curse. Medusa had been beautiful, but she was not immortal. When she and Poseidon defiled Athena's temple, Athena punished Medusa by making her even more hideous than her monstrous sisters. Her ugliness, though, went further than even Athena might have believed, for the sight of Medusa irreversibly turned anyone except her own sisters into pure stone. Many nymphs had been Medusa's victims, and the survivors were only too happy to help Perseus to fulfill his quest.

To aid Perseus, the nymphs gave Perseus several magical items to add to the gifts of Hermes and Athena. First, they gave him winged sandals just like the ones that Hermes wore. To reach the Gorgons, he would need to traverse areas that no land-bound man or beast could navigate. Next they gave him a cap of invisibility. This would come in handy after he had slain Medusa because the Gorgons could fly, and the winged sandals would not be swift enough to escape their terrible clawed fingers. Finally, they gave Perseus a magic bag. This is where he could safely store Medusa's head. Even after her head was separated from her body, Medusa's visage would still have the power to turn living creatures into dead stones. Perseus would have to be extremely careful with it, and the bag – unbreakable and opaque – would be the only way he could safely carry the awful prize.

Once he had been acceptably accessorized, Perseus asked the nymphs for the location of and directions to Medusa's lair. They gave him the information and all of their blessings. Hermes, too, blessed Perseus and shook his hand.

"Farewell," Hermes said to Perseus. "From this moment on, you are on your own."

Medusa stirred from her restless sleep and surveyed the cave. The sound of a footstep had awakened her and the multitude of venomous snakes that sprouted hair-like from her head. The snakes too were scanning the chilled darkness of the cave seeking out the intruder, but they could find none. Medusa turned her dreadful gaze toward her sisters. The other two Gorgons, Stheino and Euryale, were fast asleep against the cold stone walls of the cave. Near them lay the bloody remains of a sea bird that they had caught in the air and eaten alive for dinner. Medusa scowled at her sisters' savage appearance. She had never cared that her sisters were immortal and she originally had been mortal because Medusa had been beautiful, and that, to her, had always been a fair trade off. Now, because of Athena, she was more horrible to behold than Stheino and Euryale. With her face distorted and snakes in place of long, golden locks of silky hair, Medusa was more of a monster than they were. The only pleasure she had left in life was turning intruders to stone, and she hoped that someone was lurking about right now.

The snakes on Medusa's head turned toward the mouth of the cave in unison, their forked tongues flicking away madly. They had sensed something, perhaps the source of the sound that had woken her. She grasped the crags of the cave wall and lifted herself up quietly. She slowly and quietly crept toward the opening of the cave, her snakes sickly hissing atop her head.

Dawn sent a misty pink radiance across the lost wastes of Medusa's realm. In the half-light she was just able to make out a silhouette near the entrance of the cave. Was it a man? She could not tell. The shape was very still and hunched over. Perhaps it was just one of the many statue-victims petrified in an everlasting pose of abject horror. Medusa advanced. If the shape was, in fact, a human being, he would not live long once he looked upon her visage.

As the Gorgon got closer, the shape moved. It was a man! The snakes on Medusa's head writhed with delight. Another victim awaited her perverse stone garden.

"Sisters!" Medusa called out. "We have company!"

The figure lunged forward. Medusa laughed and waited for the man to turn to stone, but he kept on moving. He seemed to be looking at his shield.

Medusa's eyes widened. A red flash – a sword against the dawn! Searing pain, and then –

Stheino and Euryale screamed wildly at the sight of their sister being decapitated. They watched in complete shock as the intruder picked up Medusa's head by its snaky locks and tossed it into a bag. The Gorgons charged after the man, their claws extended, their bloody fangs dripping with saliva.

The man suddenly took flight. This had not been expected, but the Gorgons had wings of their own and spread their leathery appendages outward, soaring after the murderer. The mortal's miniscule winged sandals were slow compared to the flight of the Gorgons. They lashed with their claws at the air near the mortal's legs. They were nearly upon him!

And then, he was gone. The Gorgons spun wildly in the early morning sky. The intruder had placed something on his head and just vanished. Stheino and Euryale searched and searched, but all was in vain. He was gone with the head of their sister.

Meanwhile, unbeknownst to the Gorgons high above, the body of Medusa began to stir. Out of the open neck of the monster emerged her unborn children, the progeny of her defiling act with Poseidon in the temple of Athena. First, there was Chrysaor, a strange horse-like beast. Then came Pegasus, a white stallion with wings as white and as beautiful as the Gorgons' wings were black and hideous. The two offspring had been trapped in the body of their mother since her transformation. When their eyes had adjusted to the light of day and they escaped the accursed realm of the Gorgons, they went out into the world never knowing whom to thank for their freedom.

The winds buffeted Perseus mercilessly on his way back to Seriphos. He struggled to maintain the accuracy of the direction of his flight, but the exertion proved to be too much. He knew that it would be foolish to fly through the storms, for his magical sandals were powerful enough to support him but seemed strained under the weight of the current effort. More than that, if Perseus should lose control and fall into the ocean, the head of Medusa might be lost at the bottom of the sea forever. He needed to land, to wait out the storm.

In an area far west of the civilized world, Perseus came to rest upon the realm of Atlas, the son of the Titan Iapetus and brother of Prometheus. Atlas held sole domain over the land, and he was known to despise trespassers. A herd of many cattle was his to cultivate. He also owned a golden tree, which he was certain, was going to be stolen by a stranger. As Perseus landed upon Atlas's shores, he immediately approached the giant and asked permission to stay.

"Thief!" cried Atlas. "Come to steal my possessions? I shall crush you!"

Though Perseus denied the accusation, Atlas refused to listen. He slammed his fists into the ground, just missing Perseus who had soared upward just in time. The flight, though, was not swift enough, for the giant was able to swat Perseus from the sky as if he was a gnat. Grounded and dazed, Perseus was now vulnerable to Atlas's crushing blows. As the giant raised his fists above the helpless Perseus, the hero pulled out Medusa's head.

Atlas froze. His body instantly became stone at the sight of the Gorgon's gaze. Atlas toppled over and his gigantic, petrified body became the mountain range of the west.

Perseus rested before his journey continued.

The skies were much more calm now, and the magic sandals were admirably performing the task of flying Perseus home. Soon, he would be back on Seriphos and he would be able to present King Polydectes with the object he so desired. Perseus smiled, but the grin did not last long. What was it that Hermes had said about the task given to him by the King? Perseus could not remember exactly what the god had told him and the nymphs, but Hermes had certainly implied that Polydectes had given Perseus the assignment for reasons other than what it seemed. Perseus, though, could not fathom the sort of ulterior motive that Polydectes might have. If Polydectes wanted to send Perseus on an impossible mission, what would the King gain by it?

Before Perseus could continue this line of reasoning, an unbelievable sight caught his attention. A beautiful young woman was chained to a rock in the middle of the ocean. Nearby, just beneath the waves, something was lurking. Something huge.

"Who are you?" Perseus called out to the woman. "Why are you bound to this rock?"

The girl looked up at Perseus, stunned at the sight of the handsome hero flying through the sky. "Are you a god? Have you come to take me to the Underworld?"

"No. I am Perseus, son of Zeus. I am making my way back home using the gifts of those greater than myself. I ask you again, fair lady, why are you bound so?"

"I am…I was the Princess Andromeda. My mother, Queen Cassiopeia, offended the old sea god Nereus by claiming that she was more beautiful than his daughters, the Nereids. He sent a sea serpent to attack our kingdom in Ethiopia. It has come nearly every day, destroying ships and devouring our people. The oracle of the god Ammon told my father, King Cepheus, that the only way to appease Nereus and the sea serpent was by sacrificing me to the monster. That is why I am here." The girl began to cry. "Oh, please, brave hero, slay me quickly while there is time! I do not wish to die in the jaws of the monster or be dragged into its domain to be drowned before it feeds on me! Kill me, son of Zeus!"

"Never!" Perseus screamed. The water beneath him began to bubble; the lurking shape of the sea serpent grew darker and larger. "You shall not be sacrificed so unjustly, Andromeda! I will save you and take you as my bride, and you will never know such cruelty again!"

"Perseus!" Andromeda screamed. "The monster!"

The sea serpent reared its long, spiny head out of the water just behind the flying hero. It was tremendous! The serpent's mouth was elongated and narrow, ridged with rows and rows of sharp teeth. Its long neck and broad, muscular body were slick and black, covered completely by a scaly surface. As the monster raised itself out of the sea, it immediately turned its attention toward Perseus, knowing that the floating figure was hovering in its way, blocking the path toward its main meal.

The serpent struck first, opening its mouth wide in an effort to swallow Perseus whole. The hero's sandals whisked him upward out of the path of the treacherous jaws. The creature, unnaturally speedy, lunged again, twisting its head around on its serpentine neck. It snapped viciously at Perseus's feet, just narrowly missing him.

Perseus tossed the magic bag onto the beach, unsheathed the curved sword of Hermes, and then plummeted toward the base of the sea serpent's neck. The sword cut into the monster's scaly flesh, releasing a spray of thick red blood.

Howling, the sea serpent lunged at Perseus again. This time, the hero did not attempt to dodge the assault; he leveled the blade in front of him and swung with all of his might.

The monster screamed as its right eye exploded in a gush of putrid, white slime. It madly thrashed about in the foaming seas, frustrated by its enemy and in horrible pain from its wounds, but would not cease its battle with the flying man. The pain had enraged it all the more, and the sea serpent began blindly chomping at the sky.

The monster's teeth never found their mark, but the sword of Hermes did. Perseus struck at the sea serpent over and over, inflicting one gaping wound after another. The sea was filled with its blood. The monster, though, would not retreat.

Perseus did not slow his attacks. He continued slicing away at the sea serpent until the creature's neck was a mass of exposed gore. The sea serpent, bloody and blind, wretched over then stiffened, and then it fell dead into the water. Its body sunk to the bottom of the ocean, but its blood tainted everything. From that day forward, that body of water became known as the Red Sea.

Once the sea serpent had been vanquished, Perseus released Andromeda from her chains and carried her back to her father. King Cepheus was overjoyed to see his daughter again. He begged her to forgive him for leaving her to die, but Andromeda told her father not to concern himself with the matter; she had always known that he had ordered her sacrifice with the utmost reluctance.

Perseus returned to the beach to retrieve the magic bag. Some of Medusa's blood had seeped out and been absorbed by some of the surrounding sea plants. The plants became as hard as stone, and, one day, naiads would call this "coral" because, when these plants are returned to water, they become soft again.

King Cepheus welcomed Perseus to his kingdom and gladly consented to the marriage between the noble hero and his daughter. The festivities would commence immediately, for this was a day of liberation as well as celebration.

During the ceremony, a boisterous crowd entered the temple and interrupted the proceedings. The leader of the group was Phineus, Andromeda's former suitor. He claimed that Perseus had no right to marry the Princess because she had already been promised to him. Phineus, of course, had forgotten all about Andromeda once she had been chosen for sacrifice, but now that she had been safely returned, he wanted her for himself, and his band of cutthroats was going to help him get her.

Phineus's men attacked Perseus with arrows, swords, and spears. The hero defended himself with a might that only could have come from the son of a god. Some of Cepheus's people tried to aid him, but Phineus's men were prepared to slaughter them. Perseus could not allow this to happen to innocents, but he could not protect himself, Andromeda, and everyone else in Cepheus's court from the onslaught of Phineus's small army with just his sword. He tossed the sword to the side and abruptly cried out, "Friends of Cepheus, cover your eyes!" He swiftly removed Medusa's head from out of the magic bag and held it before his attackers. Phineus and his cutthroats were instantly turned to stone, and Perseus had saved Andromeda again.

Once the ugly statues had been cleared out of the temple, the ceremony continued.

"Why isn't she here?" bellowed King Polydectes to his court. "This isn't a very big island!

"Sir, you see, we…"

"No more excuses! I want my bride!" Polydectes banged his fist upon his throne, punctuating the command.

"Sire, she did reject your proposal. Perhaps we should find you someone more suitable…more willing."

Polydectes rose from his throne. "I asked her for her hand as a formality, you fool. It didn't matter what she said. Danaë should be mine right now, but you imbeciles keep losing her. We know my brother has hidden her somewhere on Seriphos because his boat hasn't left the island. Go out and find her! I want to know where she is!"

"She's hiding in the temple of Athena on the other side of the island," said a strange voice.

"Excellent!" cried Polydectes. "Now, if you'd just go and – Wait. Who said that?"

Perseus emerged out of thin air as he removed the magical cap. "I did. Do you remember me?"

The King squinted at the intruder, and then laughed nervously. "Well. Danaë's son. I remember you."

Perseus moved forward. "I found my mother. Dictys had cared for her and kept her away from you and your men, once he realized what you were after. I never knew it, but that was why you wanted me out of the way, and that's why you sent me on an impossible task. You were after my mother all along."

Polydectes made a hand gesture to his guards. They all unsheathed their swords. "Honestly, boy, it was nothing personal," the King said offhandedly. "I just didn't want somebody else's son laying claim to what would eventually belong to my true sons."

Perseus smiled. "Not even Zeus's son?"

"Zeus's son? You're Zeus's son? Ha! Impossible!"

"No, Polydectes, it isn't impossible. And neither was getting the head of Medusa." With that, Perseus removed the severed head from the bag and cast its gaze before the king, his guards, and the entire court. Within the briefest of moments, the entire corrupt government of the island of Seriphos was stone dead.

Good Dictys was soon installed as the new king of Serphos. The people were very happy to be rid of Polydectes. The citizens begged Perseus to stay, but he could not. After his mother had told him about the incomprehensible deeds of Acrisios, he had to go back to Argos and make everything right. Perseus returned the sword, sandals, bag, and cap to Hermes and he gave Athena the head of Medusa. The goddess mounted the now disenchanted head upon her terrible aegis. Perseus, Andromeda, and Danaë then made their way back to Argos.

Once there, they learned that Acrisios had given up his fight against his brother Proetus and had virtually disappeared. The rumor was that an oracle had told him something so terrible that it had plagued him to the point of madness. Acrisios had fled to Larisa, but few had even seen him. Perseus made his way there.

Once at Larisa, Perseus was able to find Acrisios in the most unfortunate manner. While there, Perseus was asked to join in public games because of his strength and stature. The champion did so, and excelled at most events. When he threw the disc, he overshot his mark, and the heavy object entered the crowd. The disc struck and killed an old man who had been watching Perseus carefully. That old man had been Acrisios. After all of these years, the oracle's prediction had finally come true.

The myth of Perseus is one of the few hero stories in classical mythology that ends happily for the main character. Perseus has married a beautiful princess, he has rescued his mother, and he has slain a number of terrible monsters while embarking on a treacherous quest. Evil in many forms is vanquished, and the will of the gods is done along the way. In the future, Perseus will become the founder of Mycenae and will rule wisely. He remains one of the most beloved characters in all of mythology.

The same cannot be said for his contemporary, Bellerophon. Bellerophon, though a successful hero, falls prey to weakness, as do so many other heroes in classical mythology. His story is directly related to the saga of Perseus, featuring similar themes, impossible quests, and a backdrop originating in the Acrisios/Proetus rivalry. Bellerophon's story also heralds the return of Pegasus, the offspring of Medusa. Where had the fabled winged stallion flown to after Perseus had decapitated the Gorgon?

For better or worse, Bellerophon knew that answer...

BELLEROPHON

In Corinth, there lived a young man named Bellerophon who claimed to be the son of the sea god, Poseidon. Bellerophon was an expert horseman, gifted in riding and taming the wildest of steeds. In recent days, many of the people of Corinth had claimed that they had seen a winged horse flying through the skies or grazing in the fields. Bellerophon was not sure if he could believe such sightings. Nevertheless, the notion of riding a flying horse captured his imagination, and it was all that he could think about for many days.

One morning, there was a flurry of activity centered near to where Bellerophon lived. He awoke and followed the rumblings of the people mobbed near his home. Bellerophon joined the crowd and asked why they had gathered. The people pointed toward Pirene, the most important spring in Corinth. There, lapping up the spring's water, was the most incredible steed Bellerophon had ever seen. It was broad and strong, and its coat was of the purest white. The horse's back was covered in gossamer feathers, the folded position of the creature's magnificent wings. The people knew that Bellerophon was one of the most skillful horsemen in all of Greece and they urged him to approach the stallion. He did so, but as he came close to the horse, the creature became frightened. It spread its wings and flew quickly away.

For all of his experience, Bellerophon was unsure how best to capture the stallion, so he went to the wise man Polyidus for advice. The seer reminded Bellerophon that, even though mankind has Poseidon to thank for the gift of the horse, it was Athena who taught man how to harness the creature and ride it. Polyidus suggested that Bellerophon spend a night in

Athena's temple in Corinth. Perhaps the goddess might come to him and tell him what to do to tame this most remarkable horse.

Bellerophon heeded the wise man's advice. That evening, he slept in the temple on the cold, stone floor. In his dreams, Bellerophon heard the voice of the goddess. She told him that the name of the creature was "Pegasus" and that he ought to be the rightful rider of the stallion. Pegasus, she told him, was related to Bellerophon in many ways, but the goddess was vague in explaining what she meant. Athena promised that when the young man awoke, he would have the solution to his dilemma. The next morning, the solution was indeed there. Athena had left Bellerophon a golden bridle, rich with the goddess's enchantments. Bellerophon gave praise to Athena, took the bridle, and then went back to Pirene to wait for Pegasus.

In a few hours, Pegasus returned for another drink. Holding the golden bridle out, Bellerophon approached. This time, the horse did not try to escape. In fact, Pegasus seemed to welcome the golden bridle. In no time, Bellerophon was able to secure the bridle, mount the horse, instruct Pegasus to trot and gallop, and then nudge the magical creature to take to the skies.

The flight was incredible. All in Corinth were astounded to see the control that Bellerophon was able to gently exert over Pegasus, thanks to his horsemanship and the golden bridle. Together, they were an awesome pair. Pegasus was powerful, majestic, and graceful, and Bellerophon looked noble and heroic atop the steed. For many days, they practiced flying over the homes and fields of Corinth so that both rider and mount might better get used to one another.

Soon, Bellerophon prompted Pegasus to fly out further away from home. This seemed not to trouble the winged horse one bit. Pegasus had an enormous amount of energy and, Bellerophon was certain, the horse could probably fly for a very long time before ever tiring. For this first outing, though, Bellerophon decided to only goes as far as Argos.

The King of Argos was Proetus, a man who had struggled his entire life against his brother Acrisios for rulership of Argos. Acrisios appeared to have mysteriously given up possession of Argos, and that allowed Proetus and his allies from Lycia to easily take over. However, Proetus's time as ruler had been full of disappointments. First, he had to spend months routing out groups of his brother's loyal supporters. Then, his daughters went mad and thought themselves cows. A hefty portion of his kingdom was subsequently given away to resolve that problem. It seemed that Proetus was fated for constant failure even when he had finally won Argos. What Proetus needed was a blessing of some sort to enhance his reign. When Bellerophon appeared in Argos, the King believed this was just the sign that would signal the beginning of his good fortune.

Bellerophon and Pegasus were welcomed to Argos in the most regal of fashions. Proetus bestowed all the hospitality to the horseman that his kingdom could provide. Pegasus, too, was given the finest of the royal stalls. Bellerophon enjoyed all of the attention and eagerly accepted an invitation to dine with the King and the Queen.

After the feast, Bellerophon was offered the most lavish accommodations for the evening. As Bellerophon prepared to go to sleep, Proetus's wife, Queen Stheneboea entered his room. The Queen made it very clear that she had been impressed by the young man's abilities and…appearance. She lunged at Bellerophon in a passionate frenzy, but the young man had the sense and willpower enough not to dishonor himself or his host. He firmly rebuffed Queen Stheneboea's advances and asked her to leave his room.

Stheneboea exited the room angrily, unused to not getting what she wanted. When she returned to her husband's chambers, she told Proetus that it was Bellerophon who had made the unwanted advances on her. Proetus received the news most dreadfully. He was tired of everything going wrong for him and he wanted to do something about this terrible disappointment. He could have ordered Bellerophon killed, but the gods looked harshly upon hosts who did injury to their guests. There was, however, another way.

The next morning, Proetus asked Bellerophon to perform for him a special service crucial to the well being of Argos. An important message had to be delivered to Proetus's father-in-law, King Iobates of Lycia, but Proetus feared that it would not arrive in time. He asked Bellerophon if he and Pegasus could fly the note there. Bellerophon was glad to perform the need. He took the coded message, mounted Pegasus, and flew off to Lycia.

The message was in a Lycian code and it explained to King Iobates the accusation of Stheneboea, his daughter. When Bellerophon arrived in Lycia, Iobates read the note and took its contents very seriously. However, by the time he was able to do anything about it, Bellerophon had already been welcomed into his kingdom and his home, and, just like Proetus, Iobates did not want to be a murderous host. Still, he had to make this vile rogue pay for what he had done to his precious daughter. He would just have to find some other entity to do the job for him. That was when the King decided to send Bellerophon out on an impossible mission.

In a mountain in Lycia, there lived a fire-breathing monstrosity called the Chimaera. It was the offspring of Typhos and Echidna. The Chimaera was a gigantic lion with the added heads of a goat on its side and a serpent for a tail. Each of the three heads could spit fire and each of the three heads loved devouring Lycians. None of the King's knights could ever get close enough to the monster to even give it a scratch. Either the knights were burned alive or they were swallowed whole. The King asked Bellerophon if Pegasus might afford him some advantage over the Chimaera. Bellerophon was not sure, but he was eager to try.

Holding the golden bridle tightly, Bellerophon guided Pegasus to the lair of the Chimaera. The huge monster was indeed a frightening thing. It roared, bleated, and hissed sparks toward the hero and his mount, but because Pegasus was so high above it, the Chimaera's mouths, claws, and flames could not reach it. Bellerophon began shooting arrows at the Chimaera. Normally, arrows would not have reached the creature because they would have been fired from the ground at a distance that was safe for the archer but was, simultaneously, an insurmountable distance. Bellerophon was firing from above, and the arrows only increased in speed and deadliness as they plummeted toward their target. Though it took dozens of arrows to finish off the beast, Bellerophon was able to slay the Chimaera and return to Iobates victorious.

The King was genuinely impressed by the deed, but disappointed that Bellerophon had survived. He decided to send the hero after another foe. This time, Iobates dispatched Bellerophon and Pegasus to drive off the Solymi, a tribe of savage warriors who had recently begun making threats to the outer parts of Lycia. Bellerophon and his winged horse engaged the enemy just as they had the Chimaera. The Solymi went off running, vowing never to return.

Iobates was beginning to like the boldness of Bellerophon. The hero had already eliminated two of Lycia's greatest enemies. It was a shame that the young man had to die. As much as it pained him, the King sent Bellerophon out on yet another impossible mission. Now he wanted the young man to defeat the Amazons, those warrior women of Asia Minor. If Bellerophon proved successful in this endeavor, though that was unlikely, he would be met upon his return to Lycia by a contingent of the King's most powerful knights. Bellerophon would never survive the double conflict.

Not that surprisingly, he did. The Amazons had been dealt a serious blow to their forces, and the knights of Lycia were all defeated. Iobates could no longer ignore the greatness of Bellerophon. He decided to ignore the request of Proetus and he gave Bellerophon his other daughter's hand in marriage. Someday, the kingdom of Lycia would be his.

For many years, Bellerophon enjoyed the fame and respect that had come with the heroic feats he had performed with Pegasus. He never knew that they had all originated out of a plot to cause his death. As time passed, though, he began to believe too much in the worshipful words of the people of Lycia. The greatness that they saw in him he began to see in himself. As the master of Pegasus, Bellerophon believed that he should not only be a regent of Lycia but also a god of Olympus. One day, he left behind his loving wife and children, mounted Pegasus, and soared off to Mount Olympus to take his place among the gods. Unfortunately, Olympus did not receive him.

Some said that it was Pegasus who had thrown Bellerophon from his back when they flew too high. Others believed that Zeus had struck Bellerophon with a lightning bolt for the hero's presumptuousness. Whatever the case, Bellerophon fell to the earth and just barely survived.

Pegasus was accepted into Olympus and the steed became the bearer of Zeus's lightning bolts. Bellerophon spent the rest of his days wandering the world as a madman, destined to die alone and almost forgotten.

The Great Heroes – Hercules, Jason, Theseus, and Meleager

With the model of the great Perseus from which to draw inspiration, the Great Heroes were prepared to accomplish deeds even more bold, daring, and dangerous than the legendary slayer of Medusa. It would stand to reason that these heroes, who lived a few generations after Perseus, would improve upon the model, but although these men left a slew of monster carcasses in their wake, all of them ultimately ended their lives in shame or despair. What caused the unpleasant turns of fortune that marred the otherwise noble and virtuous careers of men as great as Hercules and Jason?

Women.

The role of women changed dramatically for this generation of heroes. Whereas Perseus enjoyed the grace and strength of his mother Danaë and his wife Andromeda, the Great Heroes suffered because of the involvement of women in their lives. Though some of these women were actually extremely helpful to the heroes during their adventures, each lady was unquestionably the catalyst or cause of each respective man's downfall. It could easily be argued that if the heroes had not become involved with any women at all then they might always have known glory. However, that argument is an oversimplification of all of these myths.

Without the assistance of a woman, Jason, Theseus, and Meleager would never have been able to successfully complete the tasks for which they would someday become famous. Without the tragic death of Megara, Hercules would never have lived the glory of his Twelve Labors. It is necessary to discard the notion that the men of this era, or any era, would have been better off without female companionship. What we must acknowledge is not so much that a woman's involvement leads to the downfall of a man, but, rather, that a woman's involvement leads to the downfall of a hero – if he is not careful. In all cases, had the hero been more perceptive to the swirl of circumstance around him, he might have been able to undo the chain of events that would lead to his own demise. The hero had to know when to stop being a hero and just be a man.

The Great Heroes symbolized the potential of the male youth. They were capable of amazing feats and would enjoy their greatest accomplishments early in life. Later in life, though, the Great Heroes would make terrible husbands and lovers. Poor judgment, ignorance, and senseless violence seem to abound during times when there were no monsters to slay and heroes were committed or desired commitment to women. It is difficult to articulate a single lesson from the varied disappointments of these noble warriors, but it is possible to generally conclude that the wild spirit of the adventurer does not understand life when the adventure has ended.

Hercules was certainly guilty of possessing this character flaw, among others. His was a career built upon brashness, impetuosity, insensitivity, and madness. Though renowned for his incomprehensible physical strength, Hercules was feared for his small-mindedness and quick temper. His friend Theseus was a man of intelligence and great leadership potential, whereas Hercules could barely control himself. His life was one of perpetual combat, and a man such as this can never be satisfied with a sedentary lifestyle. With a mentality that was raw and primitive, Hercules would prove to be the ultimate scourge of evil, but a failure in ordinary society.

Hercules was the son of Zeus and the beautiful mortal woman, Alcmena. While Alcmena's husband, General Amphitryon of Thebes, was off to war, Zeus came to her in Amphitryon's appearance. The deception was discovered not long afterwards and was proven when Hercules was still an infant. One night while baby Hercules rested in his crib, jealous Hera sent two serpents to kill the infant child of her wayward Zeus. Alcmena and Amphitryon discovered the slithery invaders when they found baby Hercules casually strangling the snakes, one in each tiny hand. From that display of godly strength, Alcmena and her husband were certain who the father was.

Because he was the "son" of a general, Hercules was expected to endure the same sort of rigorous educational training as other sons of nobility. However, learning anything proved to be the biggest challenge of Hercules' life. He was impatient and easily frustrated by his lessons. Young Hercules had no interest in becoming academic in any sense of the word. Unless the training included swinging clubs, shooting arrows, or running through fields, Hercules cared not a whit. He especially hated the arts. While being trained to play the lyre by the famed musician Linus, Hercules became so aggravated by the lesson that he impulsively slammed the musical instrument over his teacher's head. The poor man was instantly killed.

For this, his first of many thoughtless offenses, Hercules was required to pay some price. For the death of Linus, Hercules was relegated to the status of a shepherd, a punishment that would have ordinarily shamed the son of a general. Hercules actually flourished in the role. During his time tending the cattle and flocks, Hercules gained a reputation for being able to slay wild predators with his bare hands. He would deliberately stroll through the wildest of forests in the hope of crossing paths with a lion or similarly savage creature.

During his tenure as shepherd, Hercules' impulsive nature actually became the cause of a massive war. The Minyans were exacting a yearly tribute of one hundred heads of cattle from the people of Thebes that had to be met or the Minyans threatened to slaughter Thebes' citizens. When the representatives of the King of the Minyans came to collect the tribute, Hercules would not allow them to take any cattle from his herd. He severely beat the representatives and sent them home a bloody mess. The Minyans responded by mobilizing their army. The people of Thebes were terrified, but General Amphitryon, now supported by a shepherd who was stronger than any living creature on earth, was able to repel the attackers and end the intimidation of the Minyans forever. Hercules became a national hero, having nearly defeated the entire army single-handedly.

As a reward for his performance in battle, the King of Thebes – who seemed to have forgotten that it was Hercules who had started the war itself – offered the hand of his daughter Megara to Hercules. The hero accepted and he and Princess Megara were wedded almost immediately.

There is little evidence to tell us just what sort of husband Hercules was to Megara, but we know that he did not spend much time at home. While he was married, his recognition spread throughout Greece because of the amazing deeds he had accomplished near to and far from Thebes. Most of these deeds are unknown to us today, but they had to have been suffi- ciently outstanding because they eventually captured the attention of Hera. The Queen of Olympus still harbored enormous hatred toward the mortal Alcmena's son, and that hatred swelled as Hercules' reputation grew. Hera doubted that she could exact her revenge in a physical sense against a half-god that had exhibited feats of godly strength, so, instead, she attacked his mind. Hercules, who had never cultivated his intelligence, was susceptible to mental attack, and Hera exploited this vulnerability by inflicting him with a madness made all the more violent by Hercules' own natural impulsiveness. Hercules easily succumbed to this terrible rage and, by the time the madness had passed, he had brutally slain his wife and three children.

Theseus, the Athenian hero, comforted Hercules after the murders and convinced the unintentional murderer that what had happened could not have been his fault. Originally, Hercules wanted to commit suicide, but

Theseus believed that such an act was far too impulsive and completely unjust. Instead, Hercules consulted the oracle at Delphi to ascertain the degree to which he was guilty of this horrific crime. The oracle admitted that Hercules had not been fully responsible for his actions, but that his disposition made the tragedy all the more easily perpetrated. He could not be entirely forgiven without offering some sort of tangible penance. In order for Hercules to be purified of this deed, he was to serve for ten years under the dominion of his cousin King Eurystheus of Mycenae. At the King's discretion, Hercules was to perform ten heroic acts that would demonstrate his penitence and reestablish his greatness.

Unbeknownst to the hero, his cousin was a devout follower of Hera. The goddess had been responsible for hastening the birth of Eurystheus to ensure that he would be the monarch of the region. This hastening though had resulted in Eurystheus's frail and sickly physical state. Jealous of Hercules' strength and constitution and loyal to the mandates of Hera, Eurystheus was perhaps the worst person to whom Hercules could ever have been bound. Yet, that was the situation, and simple-minded Hercules obeyed unquestioningly. The end result was the performance of twelve heroic acts that did not, as Hera had hoped, lead to Hercules' humiliation or demise. The twelve labors made Hercules more popular than ever.

THE TWELVE LABORS OF HERCULES

The Nemean Lion

In Nemea there prowled the countryside a ferocious beast of incalculable savagery. It was a lion, larger than any other, with a hide impervious to all weaponry. The beast was either the offspring of Typhos and Echidna or of their child, the Chimaera. The claws of the Nemean Lion were capable of ripping through the toughest of exteriors, shredding through even the best-made shields. To Nemea, Eurystheus dispatched Hercules, hoping that the hero would be frightened off by this terrible foe.

Hercules, who was used to killing beasts with his bare hands, was not at all daunted by the assignment. He traveled to Nemea and walked straight into the Nemean Lion's cave. The creature lunged at Hercules, baring its razor fangs, but missed its target. Hercules grabbed the lion by the waist and squeezed with all his might. Knowing there was no way he would be able to penetrate the monster's flesh, Hercules opted to crush the life out of it. The strategy worked. Within minutes, the godly strength of Hercules had defeated the lion. Using the lion's wickedly sharp claws, Hercules skinned the beast and made a dressing out of its hide. Though some claim it was the hide of the Thespian Lion that Hercules wore, most agree that it was the Nemean Lion's hide that would become the hero's fashion trademark.

The Lernaen Hydra

Another one of the children of Typhos and Echidna figured into the tasks of Hercules. This time it was the Lernaen Hydra. The hydra was a terrible snake creature that lived in the swamps of Lerna. The hydra had nine heads. The center head was immortal and very difficult to injure. The other eight heads were mortal but had incredible regenerative properties. When one of the mortal heads was cut off or severely injured, two more would grow in its place. Eurystheus was sure that Hercules would become too frustrated to be able to defeat this monster.

Hercules did become frustrated when he faced the hydra, but he never gave up. He saw this creature as the greatest challenge of his life thus far and he would not allow it to win. With his unparalleled strength, Hercules swung his club and knocked off head after head of the hydra, even though new ones kept sprouting up. When at last Hercules realized that he would not be fast enough to knock off all of the heads simultaneously, he called to his nephew and companion at the time Iolaus to bring to him a hot firebrand. Once he had the firebrand in hand, Hercules was able to sear the wounds of the hydra shut every time he decapitated another vile, mortal head. In this way, the hydra was unable to grow new ones. When Hera saw that Hercules might defeat the monster, she sent a crab as a distraction to snap at his heels. This ploy was to no avail. Hercules kicked the crab away and finished off the hydra by crushing its immortal head and body under a gigantic rock – an ironic demise in its similarity to the fate of its father, Typhos.

This was a magnificent victory for the repentant Hercules, but Eurystheus would not count it among the ten labors. Because Iolaus had been of critical assistance, Eurystheus considered this cheating. Of course, he had gotten that idea from Hera.

Though the victory did not count, Hercules was able to gain something out of the fight. He had dipped several of his arrows into the hydra's noxious blood. The arrows were now coated with a poison so powerful that even a scratch from one of the tainted shafts would instantly kill a man.

The Erymanthian Boar

Since killing things was too easy for Hercules, Eurystheus now assigned the hero to bring back to the court of Mycenae the monstrous Erymanthian Boar, alive and unharmed. Hercules, too dim to realize what the labors were really about, could not understand why anyone would want a murderous creature with sword-like tusks unleashed in his kingdom, but Eurysteus, certain that Hercules would wind up inadvertently killing the beast, remained steadfast in his demands. The boar was to be brought back to the kingdom as soon as possible. Hercules obeyed.

Once Hercules had successfully tracked down the beast, he knew better than to confront it fists to tusks. A fight would only lead to the death of one of them; either Hercules would stifle his battle tactics in an effort to leave the boar unhurt and thus leave himself vulnerable, or as the physical contest became more and more severe, Hercules would find that, to ensure his survival, the boar would have to die. To forego either of these eventualities, Hercules made a ruckus and chased the boar up Mount Erymanthus. The boar, confused by the noise, kept on running all the way to the near peak of the mountain. By that time, the boar had reached the snowy cap of the mountain and, not used to the fluffy, white drifts, found itself trapped in the snow. Once stuck, the monster was easily picked up by Hercules' superior strength. Hercules carried the creature upside down all the way to Mycenae.

When Hercules was entering the Mycenae palace with the living and angry Erymanthian Boar, Eurystheus panicked and hid in a large vase. Hercules did not know where his cousin had gone and, needing a place to keep the boar, he stashed the creature in the same vase. Neither the boar nor Eurystheus were pleased to share such cozy accommodations, but eventually both were removed.

The Golden Hind of Cerynitia

In keeping with the non-killing theme, Hera told Eurystheus to assign to Hercules the capture of a creature far less rugged than the Erymanthian Boar had been. Instead of a monster, Hercules was to track, capture, and return to Mycenae a fantastic animal that was as beautiful and sacred as it was delicate. The animal chosen was a golden hind.

The golden hinds were special to Artemis, goddess of the hunt. They were the only creatures she allowed to draw her chariot. Artemis had sworn that if any harm ever came to one of these magnificent stags, she would instantly slay the perpetrator. Hera hoped that Hercules' brutish tendencies would get the better of him and cause the stag's death, but Hercules had known of Artemis's vow and resolved to act with much caution.

It took a full year for Hercules to accomplish this task. Tracking the hind had been difficult enough, but trying to tire out the mystical beast had been nearly impossible. Hercules relied on his strength and conditioning to keep him from becoming the first to tire. The chase led all across Greece and all the way to the land of the Hyperboreans. Finally, the hind was exhausted and willingly submitted to Hercules' gentle arms. Once Hercules had shown the magical creature to the amazed court of Eurystheus, he set it free.

The Stymphalian Birds

As the labors progressed, Hercules was becoming more renowned throughout the land. So far, he had been able to match the strength, speed, agility, and powers of the individual creatures he had been ordered to confront, and Hera was becoming more vexed by his successes. It seemed that when presented with a one-on-one battle scenario, Hercules was destined to be the victor. So, Hera decided to have Eurystheus order Hercules to face multiple opponents.

In Stymphalus, there had come to roost a flock of horrendous birds. The birds were carnivorous with feathers of bronze as sharp as spears. Routinely, the birds would swoop down into the village and snatch a helpless victim. There seemed little that the people could do, for what was more frightening than the claws and plumes of the hideous creatures was the amount of them. There were hundreds. Hercules was meant to drive them all away.

To secretly assist him in this task, Athena gave Hercules a powerful artifact. It was a rattle capable of creating a terrible din. Hercules came to Stymphalus fearlessly, his bow and arrows at the ready. When he arrived in the area where the birds had migrated, he shook the rattle with all his might. The birds took flight, allowing Hercules to knock back and fire arrows away with deadly accuracy. He felled dozens of the flying terrors before the rest realized that their numbers were being quickly lessened. In just a few moments, the surviving birds fled the area, never to return.

The Stables of Augeas

It appeared that Hercules might never be humiliated on the battlefield. In fact, in between many of the labors, the hero was getting involved in other scrapes that were only adding to his fame. Eurystheus was at a loss for what to do next. He was fearful of disappointing Hera; the goddess had been responsible for his ascendancy and he knew that she could easily take away all that she had given to him. Eurystheus needed to give Hercules a task that had nothing to do with monsters or fabulous creatures. He had to give him a task that was in itself humiliating.

Dung was the answer.

The stables of King Augeas of Elis were notorious for their filth. Augeas had thousands of cattle that he kept maintained in a small, enclosed area out of fear of thieves. Unfortunately, in all the time the multitude of cattle had lingered in the stables, Augeas's servants had been unable to keep up with the amount of dung produced by the beasts. The end result was a series of hills of the stuff that no mere mortal could shovel away. Eurystheus ordered Hercules to clean the stables of Augeas…in one day.

Hercules surveyed his task carefully. He had the strength to shovel the dung away, but he might not have been fast enough to accomplish the job in the time that Eurystheus had allowed. In a moment of rare cleverness, Hercules opted to use his strength not on the dung itself, but on two nearby rivers, the river Alpheus and the river Peneus. With his bare hands, he diverted the course of the rivers, aiming them right at Augeas's stables. In no time, the dung had been washed away and the task was complete.

Disappointed that Hercules had not spent the entire day up to his neck in dung, Eurystheus did not accept the labor. He argued that Alpheus and Peneus had cleaned the stables, not Hercules. Though Hercules had now accomplished six amazing feats, he had only gotten credit for four.

The Cretan Bull

The beautiful but nasty white bull that had been both a blessing and a curse to the people of Crete became Hercules' next task. The creature, huge and mad, had been ravaging the island for years. Minos, King of Crete, had upset Poseidon by not sacrificing the bull to the sea god. In retaliation for the offense, Poseidon caused several horrible events to befall Minos and his kingdom, not the least of which was the birth of the monstrous Minotaur. Theseus would be the hero engaged to cope with the Minotaur and, ultimately, the Cretan Bull, but between those two victories, it was Hercules who was the first to conquer the bull.

It took Hercules several days to subdue the beast and return it alive to Eurystheus. The most difficult part of the task was transporting the wild creature over water, but Hercules was able to manage. After Eurystheus was satisfied that the labor had been adequately fulfilled, Hercules released the bull.

The Mares of Diomedes

With the labors half complete, Eurystheus sought out new tasks that would stretch probability and the skills of Hercules to the limit. He had to find some way to defeat his cousin – for it had been the will of Hera – but thus far, Eurystheus had only served to make Hercules all the more legendary. The members of the court of Mycenae were beginning to notice a look of worry in their monarch's eyes as Hercules became more and more popular.

The next labor was a severe test suitable only for a horseman as skilled as the once noble Bellerophon. Eurystheus wanted the man-eating mares of Diomedes broken and returned to Mycenae. For Hercules, this was an assignment unlike any other because of the specialized horse-handling knowledge needed to successfully complete it…but this was knowledge that the strongest mortal on Earth did not possess.

King Diomedes of Thrace was a follower of Ares. His chief ambition was conquest, and the only things he loved more than war were his horses. Diomedes fed his four fierce and gigantic mares human flesh to make them all the more horrible when they were let loose on the battlefield. Just before a skirmish, Diomedes would let the mares starve to ensure that, once in battle, they would take as many lives of the enemies as his soldiers would. The monstrous mares were obedient only to Diomedes; no other man could approach without being devoured.

Hercules was certain that he could best the mares with his fists or club, but conquering the beasts physically would not properly satisfy the labor. He had to tame the horses. After considering the situation for a long time, Hercules became frustrated. He threatened Diomedes, but the evil King of Thrace had so much faith in Ares that he scoffed at the son of Zeus and told him that the mares would never respond to anyone but him. His patience to the limit, Hercules gave in to his ignorant rage and flung Diomedes into the mares' eating trough. Surprisingly, the horses devoured their own master. From that point on, the mares were docile. Thanks to that bit of serendipitous luck, Hercules was easily able to lead the mares to Mycenae.

The Girdle of Hippolyta

Much was made of the theft of the girdle of Hippolyta, Queen of the Amazons. It was one of several instances when the heroes of Greece went to war with the warrior women of the wildlands. Theseus had been the first to unintentionally instigate conflict when he wooed Hippolyta and had a child with her. Hercules' labor only made things worse.

Eurystheus wanted Hercules to take the fantastically jeweled gridle off the very body of the Amazon Hippolyta so that he might give the prize to his daughter. The idea of making the girdle a gift was merely a pretext; Eurystheus was certain that Hippolyta would be offended by the attempt and would unleash the whole of the Amazon nation upon the dim-witted Hercules. Surely, even someone as powerful as Hercules would not be able to withstand the onslaught.

Ironically, Hippolyta was quite smitten by the hero from Thebes. As much as she ordinarily disdained the "frailty" of men, she found Hercules to be quite the exception to the rule just as Theseus had been. Out of sight of her followers, she gladly gave to Hercules the prize that he sought. There was no struggle, no fierce battle, and not even a negotiation. The Queen of the Amazons was more the love struck teenager than a mighty warlord.

Hera became incensed by the ease with which Hercules had accomplished the task. She appeared to the Amazons in the form of one of their own and proclaimed that a man from Greece was attempting to capture their Queen. Immediately, the Amazons charged toward the beach where Hercules and Hippolyta were saying their final farewell. When Hercules saw the horde of warrior women, he believed that Hippolyta had been treacherous and he struck her hard, killing her instantly. After swinging his club into the first ranks of Amazons, Hercules quickly manned his boat and sailed away with the girdle.

The Cattle of Geryon

Geryon was the three-bodied offspring of Chrysaor, the creature that had sprung from the neck of the beheaded Medusa along with Pegasus. The three-bodied giant lived with his red cattle on an island far from Mycenae and most of civilization. Eurystheus ordered Hercules to take the cattle away from the giant and bring all of the cows back to Mycenae. Even for a man such as Hercules, this task was nearly impossible.

The cattle would have to cross vast bodies of water, and that would require a vessel of considerable strength. Hercules knew of no such ship, and he beseeched the gods for any advice. It was the sun god who heard Hercules' prayer. He gave to the strongman a wondrous ship that would be quite capable of supporting the herd.

After a long journey, Hercules arrived on Geryon's island. When Geryon saw the intruder, he sent his two-headed dog Orthos – another of the brood of Echidna and Typhon – to kill Hercules. The hero defeated the monster with ease. When Geryon himself attacked, Hercules dispatched him with one of the deadly poison arrows tinged with hydra blood. Finally unopposed, Hercules herded the cattle onto the ship and sailed back to civilization.

Once on land with the cows, Hercules had only the tedious but relatively simple task of leading the cows to Mycenae. Hera, again, intervened. The goddess sent a swarm of gadflies to sting the cattle into a frenzy. The strategy worked; all of the cows scattered across the continent. Hercules spent weeks rounding the red cows up. The work was terribly annoying, but the hero's resolve was strong. Despite the sabotage, Hercules was able to deliver all of the cows to Eurystheus. The King, troubled by his cousin's continued success, sacrificed all of the cows to Hera in the hope of appeasing her.

The Golden Apples of the Hesperides

With only two tasks left, Eurystheus became so desperate that he dropped all pretenses and ordered Hercules to bring back to Mycenae three of the golden apples of the Hesperides. Shock was the reaction of anyone who heard Eurystheus give this order. The Hesperides were the daughters of Atlas – the Titan, not the giant slain by Perseus – and they eternally tended to a garden in which legendary golden trees with golden leaves yielded golden apples, the most beautiful objects in all the world. Unfortunately for those who might seek to steal any of the golden harvest, a fierce dragon jealously guarded the trees, and the apples themselves could only be picked by an immortal. Any mortal, like Hercules, who was miraculously fortunate enough to get past the dragon would die the instant he plucked an apple from one of the golden boughs. Add to this hopeless scenario the fact that no one actually knew the location of the garden of the Hesperides, and it was easy to see why so many felt that this labor was extremely unfair.

Despite the improbable characteristics of the assignment, Hercules accepted the labor without a complaint. He first ventured to the edge of the world where Atlas held up the sky. The Titan had been punished for his role in the war against Zeus by forever being responsible for keeping the sky and the earth separated. Rarely did Atlas get visitors, so the conversation that Hercules initiated with the Titan was a welcomed one. Atlas listened to Hercules' story carefully, but frowned when he heard what Hercules had been expected to do. The labor, Atlas assured the hero, would be impossible even for the son of Zeus, but the Titan did make a suggestion. If Hercules would hold up the sky for him – a task that ought to be easy for the strongest mortal of all time – Atlas would fetch the apples for Hercules. His daughters would not deny him anything, and he would safely be able to pluck the apples and bring them back. Seeing no other alternative, Hercules accepted the offer and traded places with Atlas.

Atlas, of course, had no intention of taking back the sky. He had finally escaped his eternal punishment and wanted nothing more than to enjoy his freedom once more. Hercules was yet again a victim of his own simple-mindedness. There he stood at the edge of the world with the heaviest burden he had ever experienced heaped upon his shoulders. Atlas might never have returned. However, the Titan did not want to further incur the wrath of Zeus, so he opted to deceive Hercules for as long as possible, maintaining the hero as a willing participant. Atlas returned to the edge of the world and showed Hercules the three golden apples. He claimed that the apples were still too dangerous for Hercules to touch. To continue "aiding" Hercules, Atlas graciously offered to bring the apples to Eurystheus for the hero, insisting that he would give Hercules all the credit for the deed. Hercules thanked the Titan and wished him a good journey, but, before Atlas left, Hercules requested a brief respite from holding up the sky while he adjusted the lion skin that he was using for a pad on his shoulders. Atlas, as stupid as Hercules, took back the sky. Hercules took the three apples and quickly departed for Mycenae.

Cerberus

The final labor was the most difficult one of all. Eurystheus told Hercules to bring Cerberus, the giant three-headed dog that guarded the gates of the Underworld, back to Mycenae. Surely, this would be the deed that would do the hero in. Traveling to the land of the dead usually meant that the traveler would never return, but tangling with the most powerful of all of the offspring of Typhos and Echidna was tantamount to suicide. Still, dim Hercules, never once grasping the true nature of the tasks his cousin had given to him, accepted the challenge with his characteristic bravado and proceeded to the Underworld.

Hades appeared almost immediately upon Hercules' arrival. The god of the dead had been aware of the great hero's labors and he believed that Hercules was capable of completing this improbable task, though Cerberus had the savagery and power to wound even a god. Hades commanded

Hercules to use no weapons against his guardian; the hero would only be allowed to use his bare hands and nothing more. Hades then gave his permission for the battle between Cerberus and Hercules to begin. The souls of the dead actually shuddered.

The dog, of course, would not be easily coerced into leaving its eternal post. The struggle that ensued was a monumental one. The bowels of the Underworld shook from the sounds of Cerberus's snarling and thrashing, and many who could only hear the battle and did not know of the identity of the combatants swore that the earth was shaking apart. When the fierce fighting was finally done, Hercules had bested Cerberus and held the monster high over his head. He returned triumphantly to Mycenae and released Cerberus when Eurystheus saw for himself that the last labor had been accomplished.

His penance complete, Hercules left Mycenae, having been accorded the full expiation of the death of his wife and children. The end result of the labors was the complete revitalization of that earlier heroic reputation that had suffered so much from the tragedy ten years before. Now, all of Greece sang the praises of Hercules, and Hera brooded. Her schemes had been for nothing. To comfort herself, Hera placed most of the blame on Eurystheus. She rescinded her blessings from the King of Mycenae, and it was not long before his fortunes dried up. Pathetic and bitter, Eurystheus became a figure of infamy. The power and glory he sought would forever elude him, and he would remain ever the pitiful creature overshadowed by the victorious acclaim of his beloved cousin.

Though Hercules had put forth the effort and resolve to be cleansed of all guilt for the deaths of his wife and children, his life did not proceed peacefully once the labors were done. More battles awaited the hero, and more heartbreak as well. For three years he served Queen Omphale of Lydia as a handmaiden. Hercules' temper had caused yet another inadvertent death similar to the death of Linus, but Zeus did not let this go unpunished and he chose Omphale to do her worst to the hero. The Queen donned Hercules' lion skin and she made the hero wear women's clothes. Instead of having Hercules perform awesome labors of strength and courage, she made him cook, clean, sew, and tend to gardens. Though humiliated, Hercules accepted the sentence. He might have been thoughtless, insensitive, and easily angered at times, but when he erred, he admitted his faults. Hercules could be as repentant as the most faithful follower of the gods.

Of the many later battles Hercules fought, the two that were most noteworthy concerned enemies that were pure elemental beings. Antaeus was a savage giant whose contact with Earth granted him invincibility. Hercules defeated Antaeus by lifting him off the ground, severing the giant's contact with his elemental source of power, and breaking his neck. The second challenger was Achelous, a river god. Both Achelous and Hercules were vying for the affections of Deianara, a Caledonian princess, and the competition degenerated into a physical conflict. Being an entity of the element of water, Achelous was a natural shape-changer. This ability usually gave the river god the advantage in a fight. However, Hercules, a veteran of battles with multi-headed monsters, was hardly alarmed by the tactic. When Achelous assumed the shape of a bull, Hercules ripped one of his horns off, wounding the minor deity in a way that no mortal had ever before. Achelous accepted defeat, and Hercules won Deianara…but this newest victory would inevitably lead to Hercules' doom.

Hercules settled down with Deianara just as he had done with Megara before. Though he was committed to her, he continued adventuring, leaving Deianara alone more often than the woman preferred. One day, when they were finally together for a bit of time, the couple came upon a river that was difficult to cross on foot. A centaur named Nessus offered to carry them safely to the other side, one at a time. Though centaurs were known to be an unsavory lot, Hercules agreed and allowed Deianara to be carried over first. When the centaur reached the opposite bank of the river, he broke into a gallop, intending to steal Deianara away. Hercules could not give chase. Instead, he fired one of his poison arrows into the back of the centaur. Nessus fell to the ground. In the brief moments he had left to live, he told Deianara that his blood mixed with the hydra blood made a powerful love potion. He encouraged her to take some of the mixture and keep it safe. If ever she feared her husband might no longer love her, she could apply the blood to an article of his clothing, and the love would instantly return. Deianara heeded the advice and secreted away some of the blood before Hercules was able to get across the river to her.

Deianara became obsessed with Nessus's warning. Soon after the encounter with the centaur, Hercules was again out fighting battles, and Deianara's usual consternation became paranoia. When Hercules returned from liberating some imprisoned maidens, Deianara was sure he had fallen in love with one of them, Iole, a king's daughter. Certain that it was time to use the love potion, Deianara dipped one of Hercules' garments into the mixture and left it for him to don. The moment Hercules' skin came into caontact with the centaur/hydra blood, he screamed in agony. Nessus had tricked Deianara. The potion was in fact an intensified version of the hydra poison.

Because of Hercules' godlike strength, the poison did not kill him. It did, however, leave him in a state of perpetual agony. When she realized what she had done, Deianara killed herself. Death was also in store for Hercules, but not until he had lived many more years in continual searing pain. To avoid such torment, the hero climbed atop a funeral pyre and gave his arrows to young Philoctetes. The boy sent a fiery shaft into the wood of the pyre and, soon, Hercules was gone. Poets say he ascended into Olympus that day and even reconciled with his longtime foe, Hera.

One final great deed awaited Hercules – the battle with the Giants, the last enemies of Olympus. It is unclear whether this event occurred before or after Hercules' death, but many believe it to have taken place after the hero's glorious ascension. Having waited countless eons, the Giants had finally unified and gathered the resolve to overthrow the Olympians. The gods waged a deadly battle with their enemies and nearly lost, but it was

Athena who suggested that Hercules be pressed into service. Hercules' participation was what the Olympians needed. His power turned the tide of battle, and the Giants were finally defeated, never to walk the earth again.

As previously noted, the Great Hero's doom is always woman, and Hercules, the greatest of all heroes, was the embodiment of that tenet. Another example of this peculiar plot device, perhaps even more striking in its consequences than the final tragedy faced by Hercules, can be found in the myth of Jason and the Argonauts. Jason's tale is considered the consummate saga – possibly the greatest single adventure of all time – but it too ends in tragedy for the hero. The Great Hero is a being of adventure, and once the adventure ends and a romantic relationship begins, the hero is incapable of settling down to become an ordinary man.

JASON AND THE ARGONAUTS

Jason is dead. His song is ended. Though once favored by Hera, he has fallen and will never rise again. How do I tell his tale? How do I sing of deeds so great, of a leader so mighty, only to finish the hymn with shame and death? I am Polyhymnia, the Muse to whom it rests to explain the deepest understanding of myths to men, but even I do weep at Jason's fate.

Shall I start with his youth? With his training by Chiron? Or should I place the beginning of his tale with the first moment he sees Medea, the sorceress? Medea, his wife. His wife and his death.

No! Jason deserves more, and so do the Argonauts!

The crew of fifty heroes sailed fearlessly to Colchis from Iolcus. On board the Argo, they labored against the seas, and in faraway lands they did battle all manner of enemies. Proudly shall I leave for the world the victories of Jason and his men, lest the shame and death be all that do remain.

"I claim Iolcus!" Jason pronounced to his wicked uncle, Pelias. Pelias had usurped Jason's father, Aeson, and he was a tyrant who feared no man but he who wore one sandal. When Jason finally had faced the accursed Pelias, he was wearing one sandal.

Aeson, near death, told the immortal Chiron to care for the infant Jason, to prepare him in all ways to take back what was rightfully his. Jason learned well and became formidable in all manner of tasks. Chiron had molded him into a hero and sent him to Iolcus when he believed the young man to be ready. And ready he was! Jason's heart was afire, his blood molten with righteousness!

190

But Jason's proclamation would have meant nothing to Pelias if not for the missing sandal. An oracle had told the tyrant that the man who comes to him wearing one sandal would bring about his downfall. "Where is your sandal?" Pelias asked. Jason did not tell Pelias how he had lost it while helping an old woman cross the river Anaurus. "I claim Iolcus!" was his only reply.

Pelias convinced Jason and all of Iolcus that the son of Aeson would have to prove himself if he wanted leadership. The tyrant set him to the impossible task of recovering from faraway Colchis the legendary Golden Fleece, and Jason heartily accepted. Chiron had trained him well enough to overcome any challenge.

The call went out for heroes who would join Jason's cause. While Argos and the goddess Athena built Jason's ship, the Argo, great men from all of Greece converged upon Iolcus to become brothers to Jason in his quest. There was Tiphys, the celestial navigator; Erginus, expert in wind and water; Lynceus, whose eyes discern the farthest stars; Hercules, the strongest man in the world; Castor, the expert horseman, and his brother Pollux, the renowned boxer; Autolycus, the master thief; Orpheus, the Muses' musician; Mopsus, the prophet; Peleus, warrior of the lance; the winged sons of the wind, Calais and Zetes; Meleager, the great hunter and fighter; Acastus, slinger of javelins; and so many others of the greatest nobility. Fifty in all joined Jason in his cause, but there was another who was with Jason the entire time. It was Hera, the Queen of Olympus. She had taken the form of an old woman to test Jason's decency. He had carried her in his arms – Yes! Jason had carried the wondrous Hera, and, for such a deed, she would guide his flight always.

But, oh! How Jason did fall! Medea was to blame! It is clear. Medea does taint this tale!

No, I cannot allow it! No matter how cruel, Medea shall not taint the greatness of the deeds of the Argonauts. On the journey to Colchis, the heroes distinguished themselves magnificently, and they shall be remembered!

On Lemnos, the Argonauts tamed Queen Hypsipyle and her murderous followers who had killed all of the men on their island, save the Queen's own father. The greatness of the Argonauts awed the female marauders and made them good.

On Kyzikos, the Argonauts did battle the Gegeneis, giants born of Earth. Hercules led the attack upon the barbaric savages, all of whom were slain.

On Cios, a selfish nymph captured Hercules' companion, Hylas. Thoughtlessly, Hercules went off to find the boy and never returned to the Argo. They dared not challenge him for they knew what destruction Hercules was capable of mindlessly committing when so enraged.

On an island in the Bebryces, wicked King Amykos challenged the Argonauts to send one of their own to box with him, lest he forbid them much needed fresh water. Pollux eagerly accepted the challenge for his crewmates and his further glory. So masterful was Pollux that Amykos did not survive the fight.

On an uncharted island, the Argonauts met Phineus, a man struck blind by the gods for cruelty to his wife. Each day, when Phineus tried to eat, the foul Harpies, monstrous women-vultures, would swoop down from the mountain and steal his food. Calais and Zetes were better flyers. The sons of the wind chased the Harpies away forever. Thankful Phineus gave the Argonauts much guidance.

Through the clashing rocks, the Sympleglades, all ships were crushed, for the mountainous, moving stones waited for anything to try to get between them. Phineus told Jason to send a dove through the Sympleglades and then, as the rocks parted once more, the Argonauts must furiously row. Jason carefully heeded the advice and did just what Phineus had told him. Once the Argo was successfully through, the Sympleglades had finally failed to destroy a ship. The rocks never moved again.

Now the Argo made its way across the treacherous Black Sea passing the lands of the Amazons, the new home of the Stymphalian Birds, the

Chalybes, vicious cannibal tribes, pirates, and more. They stopped at nothing until they finally reached Colchis, the island of the Golden Fleece.

Mighty Hera had arrived at Colchis first, ordering Aphrodite to cast a spell of love upon the Colchian King's daughter that she might prove useful in the next set of Jason's trials. The spell proved successful, though many, even Hera herself, might have regretted the strategy later.

The King's daughter was Medea.

King Aeëtes of Colchis received the Argonauts coldly. He would not willingly hand over the Fleece; it was too prized a possession. The Fleece had originally been a golden ram sent by Hermes to rescue the children of Nephele. Nephele's husband, King Athamas of Thebes, had discarded her and taken a new wife, Princess Ino, one of the daughters of Cadmus. Ino wanted to be rid of Nephele's children, Phrixus and Helle, so she tainted the seeds of Thebes and claimed that the ensuing famine could only be alleviated by sacrificing Phrixus and Helle. The gods detested human sacrifice and quickly answered helpless Nephele's prayers. Hermes sent a golden ram to fly to the children and whisk them to safety. During the flight, Helle fell into the straits between Europe and Asia and drowned. Her resting place was forever known as the Hellespont. Phrixus had made it safely to Colchis and was welcomed by Aeëtes. The golden ram was sacrificed to the gods and its fleece was hung at the highest point on Colchis, ever defended by a sleepless dragon.

Sinister King Aeëtes agreed to hand the Golden Fleece to Jason if he could perform heroic tasks that would prove his worthiness. Such was the way of the tyrant – to disguise murderous intent with a call to noble deeds. Aeëtes demanded that Jason alone harness the fire-breathing bulls made of brass, plow the fields of Ares with them, sow the fields with dragon's teeth, and then defeat the men that spring up from the ground. Aeëtes knew that no man could accomplish this. What he did not know was that his daughter Medea, a powerful sorceress, had fallen in love with Jason and would do anything to help the hero.

Medea prayed to dark Hecate. With the witch-goddess's inspiration, Medea concocted an ointment that would render Jason immune to the flames of the bulls. She also received advice about how to defeat the men sprung from dragon's teeth. She went to Jason the night before his trials and gave him the ointment, the advice, and her heart. Jason promised to take her back to Iolcus with him. He would love her forever.

Oh, rash Jason! Such promises made are made too quickly! The senses do lose sight when the heart speeds ahead! I almost do not wish to mention her part in your story. Medea was a barbarian's daughter, a follower of Hecate, and the niece of wicked Circe the sorceress. And yet, without her help, you would never have survived.

Survive Jason did! He was victorious against the bulls whose flames could not hurt him. The men of the dragon's teeth were disposed of quite easily. Jason had proven his worth to Aeëtes. The King promised Jason that the Fleece would be his by the next morning. Before passing on the artifact, there would be a great feast.

Medea came to Jason during the feast and told him that her father was planning on murdering him and the Argonauts during the night while they slept. Aeëtes never had any intention of handing over the Golden Fleece. The sorceress convinced the hero that they must act quickly. They must take the Fleece and flee.

Under cover of Hecate's blackest night, Jason and his men went forward toward the highest point of Colchis. There was the Fleece and the sleepless dragon that guarded it. Medea spoke terrible arcane words, and the dragon's eyes closed in a perpetual slumber. Jason took the Fleece and all fled to the Argo.

Medea had taken her brother Apsyrtos onto the ship with them, though none knew why. As the Argo set sail, the theft of the Golden Fleece was discovered, and the army of Colchis manned their ships to give chase. Aeëtes was in the lead ship vowing to get his Fleece and his children back, for he was convinced that all had been stolen from him. When the Colchian fleet drew close enough to attack, vile Medea killed Apsyrtos, dismembered him, and tossed his remains into the Black Sea. Horrified, Aeëtes halted his fleet in an attempt to collect all of the pieces of his slain son. The Argonauts were sickened by the act, but at least they were free to return to Iolcus.

They safely survived the mesmerizing suicide songs of the evil bird-women, the Sirens, thanks to the music of Orpheus. When passing Crete, Medea's magic defeated the bronze man Talos, who flung rocks from the shore. With Hera's assistance, the Argonauts careened between the sea monsters Scylla and Charybdis and were not damaged. Upon reaching home, the Argonauts disbanded and happily left Jason to his kingdom.

When Jason presented the Fleece to Pelias, the old tyrant refused to abdicate the throne. Medea would not allow her beloved to be denied what was rightfully his. She came to the daughters of Pelias and convinced them that she knew of a magical process that would restore their aging father's youth. The girls watched in amazement when Medea proved her word on an old ram. She dismembered the creature, put it into a pot of herbs, and cast a spell of rejuvenation. The limbs reassembled and out of the pot leapt a baby lamb.

Pelias's daughters eagerly tried the process on their father. They went to him while he slept and cut him into many pieces. They put him into a pot with the herbs, but nothing happened. The process had, of course, been nothing more than Hecate-inspired trickery. Pelias was dead.

Iolcus became Jason's, though it was a rule tainted by rumors of foul black magic. For ten years, he and Medea ruled the land, but the Colchian sorceress remained often out of sight of the people of Iolcus. Medea bore Jason two children...poor, innocent sweet victims of their mother's vicious scorn. Jason, bored from the lack of adventure, tired of Medea's wicked ways, and desirous of furthering his cause, decided to marry Princess Glauke of Corinth. Hera, the goddess of marriage, abandoned Jason from that very moment, and, as it would be expected, Medea was not going to accept being rejected by the man for whom she had committed so many atrocious acts.

There is no good to come to the hero who puts his faith in woman. Medea sent a poisoned robe to Glauke who died the moment she donned the enchanted garment. The sorceress then set fire to the palace of King Creon, Glauke's father, killing him. Finally, Medea butchered her own children. She summoned a chariot drawn by dragons and soared into the clouds to find a new home for her evil.

Jason, the great hero, the courageous leader, the forge of the Argonauts, was ruined. He wandered aimlessly until he decided to return to the sight of his fondest memories. He ventured back to the Argo, which now resided in the Isthmus of Corinth. As he sat beside the ship of his former glory, a piece of the stern fell off, striking him dead.

Oh, Jason, though it is to me to tell the myths as they are, I pray to all of Olympus that the memory of your deeds outlives the tragedy that ended your noble life.

Different sources give varying accounts of what happened to Jason and Medea after the death of Pelias, but whether they were installed as royalty or exiled in shame, the end result was always the same. Medea was ultimately Jason's ruination, though many would argue that he brought the sorceress's wrath upon himself.

Thus far, all of the heroes detailed have been "assigned" the adventures that yielded them fame. In most cases, the heroes were given impossible tasks in the hope that they would not survive. The fact that these heroes did not always seek out challenges on their own did not diminish their eminence. Often, it was a sign of true greatness to "accept" a challenge not of one's own making. The one hero who diverged from the plot device of the "impossible task" was the enormously popular hero from Athens, Theseus.

So popular was Theseus that he appeared in more myths with other renowned characters than any other hero in classical mythology. The consequence of so many appearances is that chronological continuity becomes skewed in the details. As has been previously mentioned, Theseus could not have possibly appeared in as many stories as have been handed down to us today; it would be a physical impossibility for a mortal character. In all probability, he was such a beloved character to mythmakers and playwrights that it was difficult for them to resist his inclusion in their tales. Even the interconnectedness between Theseus's adventures and Hercules' labors draws attention to the storyteller's desire to raise Athens' hero to the highest pinnacle.

Theseus was not as strong as Hercules, but he was extremely intelligent and he had a code of ethics that earned him respect even from those he battled. He got the opportunity to begin his career as a hero very early in life. His father, King Aegeus of Athens, sent the infant Theseus to live with his mother Aethra in a land far from the kingdom. When the boy was old enough to move a stone under which Aegeus had hidden a sword and sandals, his son was then to be instructed to return to the kingdom. Once Theseus had grown mighty enough to heave the weighty stone aside, Aethra told him of his father and the kingdom he would inherit. Theseus was so eager to earn his way to the throne that he declined to take a ship to Athens. Instead, he decided to groom himself for heroism by making the long journey alone on foot.

During the trip, Theseus encountered and defeated several murderers and monsters, and he could not have been happier. The young man thought it best that he learn by trying, and in order to learn to be a just and mighty hero, he had to defeat evil. From common thieves to sadistic giants, Theseus defeated all of the villains that he encountered, usually by using their own evil devices or methods against them. This was the beginning of a long career of meting out fitting and appropriate justice.

When Theseus finally reached Athens, his reputation had already preceded him. Aegeus was prepared to receive with a banquet this hero everyone had heard so much about. At the banquet, Aegeus would poison the young man. He had to – his wife had told him that the unnamed hero was a dire threat to Athens.

Aegeus's wife was Medea. After fleeing the bloodshed in Iolcus and Corinth, her dragons had taken her far from Greece. Eventually, she returned to lay claim to a new kingdom. She had set her sights on Athens, the city-state that had become one of the most prosperous places in civilization, but now the return of the prince was most distressing. Medea's sorcery had shown her Theseus's true identity before anyone else knew. She had to be rid of the heir lest her plans go awry.

At the banquet, King Aegeus handed a poisoned drink to Theseus, who had yet to reveal his name. When the King saw the sword that the hero carried, he immediately knew that the person he was about to murder was his own son. He smacked away the cup and embraced Theseus.

Medea, once again, escaped.

Though Theseus had now taken his rightful place in the court of Athens, his desire for adventure and the dispensing of justice was still very much a part of who he was, more so than a mere sedentary prince. So, when the ships arrived from Crete to exact their terrible tribute from Athens, Theseus found another opportunity to act.

King Minos of Crete had threatened Athens with destruction after his son had died in the service of the Athenian King. To assuage the retribution, every nine years the people of Athens were to give to Crete seven young men and seven maidens to be delivered into the death maze of the Minotaur, a hideous abomination that was the curse of Minos. Upon hearing the tale of how young Athenians were being sent to their deaths in the lair of an unspeakable monster, he immediately volunteered to be one of the captive youths.

This adventure connects Theseus to one of Hercules' labors. The Minotaur was the offspring of the Cretan Bull and Pasiphaë, the King's wife. Minos had been given the beautiful bull by Poseidon, and then had been asked to sacrifice it. Minos refused. Poseidon made Queen Pasiphaë fall in love with the bull. After secretly going out to the bull in a cow disguise created by the brilliant inventor Daedalus, Pasiphaë gave birth to a hideous half man half bull beast that devoured human flesh. Rather than killing it, Minos insisted that Daedalus create a maze from which the creature could not escape. Daedalus's creation, the Labyrinth, was so intricate that the Minotaur would never be able to make its way out to the surface of Crete, and any victims offered to the monster would likewise be unable to escape. Poseidon, still wanting retribution, made the beautiful, tame Cretan bull mad with rage, causing it to attack anyone in its path. This was when Hercules had been summoned to capture the beast for Eurystheus. While that labor was being conducted, Theseus was facing the Minotaur.

Aegeus did not want his son to leave; they had just been reunited. Theseus was adamant. He promised to return in the black-sailed Cretan ship, but he would change the sails to white to signify his triumph.

Once on Crete, Theseus and the other captives were paraded through the city. When Princess Ariadne, the daughter of Minos, saw Theseus, she immediately fell in love. Ariadne went to Daedalus for advice about the Labyrinth. Afterwards, she went to Theseus, gave him the advice of Daedalus and a spool of thread to use to find his way back to the surface, and then kissed him goodbye.

When Theseus entered the Labyrinth, he followed Ariadne's advice and made a trail with the thread. He kept the other captives with him and when he finally confronted the Minotaur, he told the group to move to safety. Theseus, who already had experience slaying monsters, killed the Minotaur with his bare hands. He followed the thread and the advice of Daedalus and led everyone back to the surface.

Theseus took Ariadne with him, but for some reason that no sources can agree upon, he left her on the island of Naxos. The god Dionysus came to her and took her for his own. Theseus's father, however, did not meet such a favorable fate. As Theseus's ship approached Athens, it still showed the black sails instead of white. Believing his son dead, Aegeus flung himself into the sea. That body of water became known as the Aegean.

Theseus became King of Athens. Knowing that a hero's life belonged to adventure, he created civilization's first commonwealth, a government run by the people. The power of rulership now was in the hands of the citizenry. Theseus himself only wanted to retain control of the army if ever there came a time when a commander was needed. Athens prospered more than ever.

Theseus's adventures continued and so did the goodness and justice he spread throughout the world. He tracked down the mad Cretan Bull and killed it in Marathon. He accepted the exiled and shamed Oedipus when everyone else rejected him. He made peaceful overtures to the Amazons, even wooing and having a son with Queen Hippolyta, but the Amazons still attacked Attica; Theseus nevertheless prevailed. With his friend Pirithoüs, Ixion's son and King of the Lapithae, Theseus battled tribes of centaurs and journeyed into the Underworld. When Hercules came to capture Cerberus for his last labor, he rescued Theseus, who had become trapped in a mystical chair. Pirithoüs, who wanted to woo Persephone away from Hades, could not be saved.

It would seem that Theseus and his career had been spared the shame that had plagued so many other heroes, but the classical tragedians would not let him be. Later in life, Theseus finally married. His wife was Phaedra, sister of Ariadne. When Phaedra met Hippolytus, Theseus's son by the Amazon Queen, she fell madly in love with the young man. Hippolytus would not shame himself or his father by giving in to his stepmother's advances and soundly rejected her. Pained by the dismissal, Phaedra killed herself and left a note claiming that Hippolytus had mortally wounded her when she tried to fend off his advances. Discovering his deceased wife and the note, a shocked and grief-stricken Theseus cursed his son to Poseidon. Soon, the god of the seas answered the rashly spoken curse, and Hippolytus was dead. The goddess Artemis came to Theseus and told him of his tragic error. From that moment on, all was dark for the hero of Athens. The actions of Phaedra led to Theseus's exile and his eventual death at the hands of King Lycomedes, a cruel rival who took advantage of Theseus's shattered state.

Many years before the tragic end, Theseus had participated in one adventure that marked for another hero a moment that was his finest as well as his most tragic. Meleager, who had been one of the Argonauts, returned to his native Calydonia a hero. A few years later, when Meleager's father King Oeneus had offended Artemis, the goddess sent a monstrous boar of gigantic size and fearsome disposition to ravage Calydonia. Naturally, the citizens turned to Meleager. Meleager courageously accepted the challenge. He had never been defeated before and did not expect this boar to be any different.

Meleager's story is a succinct version of all that befalls the Great Hero. In one short adventure, Meleager will symbolize the triumph that comes with adventuring and the tragedy that follows the adventurer in love.

THE CALYDONIAN BOAR HUNT

Meleager unknowingly owed much of his previous successes in battle to his mother, Althaea. In a dream, Althaea had heard the Three Fates discussing her son's lifespan. For whatever reason, the length of his life had been tied to a piece of wood burning slowly on the hearth. Althaea removed the wood from the fire and kept it in a safe place. No matter how much Meleager adventured, he was indestructible so long as the piece of wood remained untouched by flames.

Against the Calydonian Boar, Meleager was quite invulnerable, but it seemed that the boar was invulnerable, too. Meleager quickly realized that he would need a force of many heroes to track, trap, and slay this beast. So the call went out to all the heroes in the land, especially Meleager's former comrades on the Argo. Many illustrious warriors including Jason, Peleus, Lynceus, Castor, Pollux, Theseus, and Pirithoüs joined Meleager, as well as a young woman named Atalanta. Though the sight of a woman at a hunt was rare, several had heard of Atalanta. She had already distinguished herself as a speedy runner and relentless huntress. When the hunt began, Atalanta was easily able to keep up with the men.

In the first few hours of the hunt, the boar's sword-like tusks gored several men, but Atalanta and Meleager remained unshaken. The more Meleager watched the huntress in action, the more he became enamored by her. When Lynceus was about to be rammed by the charging monster, it was Atalanta who finally dealt the creature a severe blow and saved the hero's life. All of the hunters were impressed. The first arrow to pierce the boar's thick hide had been fired by a woman.

Meleager, eager to win Atalanta's affections, attacked the boar with an intensity never before witnessed. His spear followed Atalanta's arrow, and it was not long before the newest wound proved fatal to the beast. When the hunt had ended, all praised Meleager and Atalanta.

Once the boar had been skinned, the hide was given to Meleager, his prize for dealing the deathblow. Meleager turned to Atalanta and offered the trophy to her. This act enraged Meleager's uncles. It was customary, they claimed, for such a prize to be given to the family or to the King, not to a wild woman of the forests. At the insult, Meleager flew into a rage. By the time the other heroes were able to calm Calydonia's champion from his frenzy, his uncles already lay dead.

Althaea received the news of the deaths of her brothers with the same insane fury. She cursed her son, removed the piece of wood from its hiding place, and tossed it into the flames of the hearth once more. When the stick had completely burned, she knew her son was dead. Althaea followed the horrid act with her own suicide.

Part 4

Other Notable Characters

Achilles

The son of Peleus and Thetis, Achilles was the great warrior upon whom the fate of the Trojan War hung. The seeds of war had been sown at the wedding of his parents, so it was quite fitting when a seer predicted that Troy would never fall without Achilles fighting on the side of Greece. When Achilles was an infant, Thetis had dipped him into Styx, the river sacred to the gods, to make him invulnerable. She had known that if Achilles ever went to war against Troy, he would die. Sadly, Thetis did not dip Achilles all the way into the river; the heel by which she held him remained exposed. During the tenth year of the Trojan War, when Achilles' pride nearly cost the Greeks victory, the Trojan Paris killed him with an arrow guided by Apollo into Achilles' vulnerable heel.

Amalthea

When the nymphs of Crete were tending to the young Zeus, the god was given the appropriate sustenance by the magical goat, Amalthea. The horns of Amalthea were a limitless supply of ambrosia and nectar, the food and drink of the gods. Amalthea's horns of plenty were also capable of producing any other kind of nourishment for any other sort of being. When the goat died, its horns continued to provide an endless menu of tasty treats.

Arachne

One of the most faithful followers of Athena, Arachne pledged her life to the art of weaving. She created tapestries of magnificent quality. After a while, her talent began to inflate her ego, and she began to believe herself a greater artist than Athena herself.

Arachne had put out the word that she was the best weaver in the land. Athena arrived to take up the challenge in the guise of an old woman.

Before the competition began, Athena questioned the youthful Arachne to see if she might repent her lamentable hubris. The girl did not, and so Athena revealed herself and, despite Arachne's shock, the contest had to proceed.

The mortal weaver attempted to distract the goddess by weaving a scene of the gods at their most lascivious. It was a scene most blasphemous, and all who looked upon it cringed in horror.

Athena's tapestry was the most elegant and sophisticated that anyone had ever seen. It depicted the majesty of great Olympus.

No judge would dare cast a ballot against Athena, but no mortal judge ever had the opportunity to speak. Athena directed her own divine judgment on the vain and insolent Arachne by transforming her into a spider, an ugly insect that would spend the rest of its days doing nothing but spinning tapestries of crude webbing.

Callisto

Callisto of Arcadia was another of Zeus's many mortal loves. To Zeus, Callisto gave birth to a son she named Arcas. Arcas grew into a fine hunter, and the two were very happy for quite some time.

When Hera discovered Callisto's identity after Zeus had paid another visit, she changed the woman into a bear, leaving Callisto a voiceless victim in the woods. Arcas was hunting at the time the transformation had taken place and had no knowledge of what had transpired. Callisto eventually encountered Arcas and she approached him, her large bear paws extended for a hug. Arcas did not know the bear was his mother and he lifted up his spear to plunge it into the heart of the approaching creature. Fortunately, Zeus intervened and carried Callisto into the heavens, making her the constellation of the Great Bear. When Arcas died, he joined his sanctified mother as the Little Bear.

Hera pleaded to Poseidon that to honor a mortal woman in such a way was an outrage. She persuaded the sea god to forbid the two new constellations from ever "falling into the ocean" as other stars did. That is why the bears forever circle around the pole.

Cassandra

One of the most tragic personalities of the Trojan War, Cassandra was the daughter of Troy's King Priam. Apollo had loved her so much that he bequeathed to her the ability to see so clearly that she could discern future events. However, Cassandra did not love Apollo in return, and this angered the god. He punished Cassandra by leaving with her the ability of prescience, but cursed her so that no one would ever believe her warnings.

Cassandra predicted all of the doom that would befall Troy, including the surprise attack from the Trojan horse. No one, not even her father, ever believed her, and Troy was obliterated.

Centaurs

King Ixion of the Lapithae was a rude and vile man. His greatest blasphemy was his desire for the Queen of Olympus. He did not respect or worship Hera; rather, he wanted her to be another one of his concubines…and he even thought that he deserved her. To test how deeply ran this desire, Zeus sent a cloud down to Ixion to see what he would do. Immediately, the unctuous King, thinking this was a manifestation of Hera, raped the cloud. For that and many other crimes, he was severely punished in the Underworld.

The mating of Ixion and the cloud produced an unexpected progeny. The cloud began to give birth to a horde of half man, half horse creatures called centaurs. The centaurs, all male, were the embodiment of Ixion's primitive and wanton behavior. They were creatures so uncivilized that often they attacked towns and carried off women for absolutely no reason and even when they would be sorely outnumbered. The essence of wildness, centaurs would be a bane to the Lapithae for decades to come.

Chiron

Chiron was a centaur, but not one from the brood that had emerged from Ixion's cloud. Chiron was an immortal descendent of Cronus. He was everything Ixion's centaurs were not – noble, kind, brilliant, and wise. Many great men of Greece, including Jason and Achilles, owed their education to the teachings of the legendary Chiron. Whereas centaurs symbolized the basest of primitive natures in man, Chiron showed that the pursuit of intelligence was the path of greatness.

Circe

A favorite of the goddess Hecate, Circe was a sorceress of incredible power. She was Medea's aunt, and could be just as cruel as her niece. Circe had a habit of turning people into beasts of all sorts, either out of pleasure or convenience. She had been responsible for changing Scylla into an abomination and, when Odysseus and his men landed in her realm on Aeaea, she turned all of them into swine. With the help of Hermes, Odysseus was able to free his men. He was the only one to ever get the better of the woman who epitomized the elemental powers of magic and night.

Deucalion

Deucalion was the son of Prometheus. When Prometheus looked into the future and saw the terrible flood that Zeus would unleash upon the corrupted men and women who had come from his clay, he warned Deucalion to take refuge. The young man obeyed and he and his wife Pyrrha hid themselves in a little boat.

The flood lasted for nine days and nine nights. When it was over, Deucalion and Pyrrha stood upon dry land and gave thanks to the gods. Zeus was so surprised that the only two remaining mortals had forsaken anger in favor of piety that he instructed them to take "the bones of the mother" and throw them over their shoulders.

Deucalion realized that Zeus was referring to rocks on the ground of Mother Earth. He and Pyrrha obeyed. For every rock they threw, a new person sprang out of the earth. These people originating from stone were more robust than the clay people and, since they were beings of the earth, would be more apt to use the gifts of Mother Earth wisely.

These were the people from whom the ancient citizens believed themselves descended.

Hecate

Hecate was the infamous goddess of night and black magic, daughter of Tartarus. It was she who was associated with the dark phases of the moon rather than Artemis who symbolized the silvery light of the gleaming orb.

As the goddess of witches, Hecate held a special place in the subculture of the pantheon of Olympus. She was feared and respected, for she could move the elemental forces in arcane ways that even the other gods could not understand. It is likely that there are virtually no full myths devoted to her because there was a real fear in her unearthly powers. It was said that even Zeus gave her latitude to do as she saw fit.

Hecate's most famous followers were Circe and Medea. If the actions of these two mere mortal sorceresses were any indication of the power and influence of Hecate, it is easy to see why the goddess of the dark arts was so dreaded.

Hero and Leander

Hero was a priestess of Aphrodite who served the goddess from her home on Sestos. Directly across the Hellespont in Abydos lived Leander, a young man of modest means. When hero and Leander had first met, they immediately fell in love. However, Hero's parents would not permit that love to blossom.

Leander would not be denied his Hero. Every night, he would wait by the shore for Hero to light a torch in the temple of Aphrodite. That would be the signal that her parents were asleep. Leander would then swim across the treacherous Hellespont to reach Sestos and spend some stolen moments with his love.

One stormy night, the lovers' desires overwhelmed good sense. Leander swam across during terrible weather. The violent winds blew out the torch and without a guiding light Leander tragically lost his way amid powerful waves. The next day, Hero found his dead body washed ashore. Soon after, she took her own life.

Icarus

After the great inventor Daedalus had betrayed the secrets of the Labyrinth to Ariadne and Theseus, King Minos of Crete locked him and his son Icarus in a high tower. Minos was sure that this would be a prison that even the ingenious thinker could not escape, but he was wrong.

Daedalus and Icarus collected feathers from birds that alighted upon their prison ledge. After they had collected a multitude, Daedalus fastened the feathers together with wax, creating two sets of giant wings. He showed his son how to use them and warned the boy not to fly too close to the sun, lest the wax melts and the wings fall apart. The boy acknowledged all of his father's instructions, and the escape was on.

As soon as Icarus began flying, the boy became filled with excitement. The warning Daedalus had given to him was quickly forgotten. The youth soared higher and higher. As Daedalus had predicted, the wax on the wings began to melt as soon as Icarus rose too close to the son. The wings fell apart, and the young man fell to his death in the ocean below.

Iris

Iris was the goddess of the rainbow and the special messenger of the gods, much like Hermes. She was also the special attendant to Hera, often doing more for the Queen of Olympus than the King.

The winged goddess was believed to be responsible for the showers that afterwards created rainbows that stretched from heaven to earth. These were the bridges she used to deliver her important missives. Iris was also associated with light and the parting of clouds. Similarly, it was believed that she had the power to bring light to the people as another sort of message from the gods. Her rainbows were always considered good omens.

Leda

Another of Zeus's dalliances, Leda was the mother of several famous children. Zeus had come to Leda in the form of a swan and ravaged the woman in his own divine way. Afterwards, Leda gave birth to four offspring, some sources claiming that the children were hatched from eggs. Leda's husband was the father of Clytemnestra and Castor, while Zeus was the father of Pollux and Helen.

Castor and Pollux would become the inseparable adventuring brothers of many tales, while Clytemnestra and Helen – yes, the Helen – would figure prominently in the story of the Trojan War. That, of course, creates some continuity errors with the ages of the siblings, for it is often considered that Castor and Pollux lived approximately one generation before the Trojan War.

Midas

One of the foolish Kings of Phrygia, Midas was famous for his golden touch. He had shown kindness to a drunken satyr who had been a devout follower of Dionysus. In return for the favor, Dionysus offered to grant Midas a single wish. The King, desiring more wealth, wished that everything he touched be turned to gold. Of course, this was an idiotic wish, and Midas prayed to have it removed lest he starve to death. Dionysus told him to bathe in the river Pactolus. The King did so, and the power was gone. The river, though, maintained some of the gold-making properties.

When another satyr entered a musical contest against Apollo, Midas acted as the judge. When the competition had ended, it was obvious to all that Apollo was the master musician. Midas, who had barely been paying attention, selected the satyr as the victor. Outraged, Apollo replaced Midas's ears with those of an ass.

Midas tried to keep his new ears a secret from his people, but he was a gossip as well as a fool. When the desire to speak of his condition could no longer be contained, he dug a hole and told the earth. The next spring, there grew from the ground weeds that whispered, "Midas has ass's ears," when the wind blew through them. The King was humiliated. He left Phrygia, never to be seen again.

Muses

The nine daughters of Zeus and the Titan Mnemosyne (also called Memory) were the inspirers of all fine arts, especially those involving writing. Almost every poet of the ancient world began his works by praising the Muses for their divine influence.

Calliope, the Muse of epic poetry and mother of Orpheus, was considered the chief Muse. Erato was the Muse of lyric poetry and ballads of love. Thalia was the Muse of comedy, and Melpomene was the Muse of tragedy. Euterpe, whose name means "giver of pleasure," was the Muse of music. Urania was the Muse of astronomy. Clio was the Muse of history. Terpsichore was the Muse of dance. Finally, there was Polyhymnia, the Muse of hymns and myths.

The Muses could often be found on various mountains, perfecting their arts. Other times they journeyed to Mount Olympus to entertain the gods. Apollo helped to train the Muses and they, in turn, went on to train Orpheus, the greatest mortal musician who ever lived.

Narcissus

Narcissus was so handsome that every woman who saw the young mortal fell in love with him. Nymphs were not immune to his appearance either; the nymph Echo took one look at the beautiful stranger and longed to be with him.

Hera cursed Echo some time before when the nymph had distracted the goddess with useless chatter while Zeus slipped off to enjoy one of his flings. As punishment, Echo could no longer form words of her own; she was forced to repeat what other people said. As the nymph came upon Narcissus by the side of a mountain stream, she longed to repeat anything the beautiful youth spoke.

Echo never got the chance. The sight of his own reflection in the water had mesmerized Narcissus. He had, in fact, fallen in love with himself.

The youth could not stop looking at his reflection. He remained there, never eating or drinking. Eventually, Narcissus died. Where he had been sitting, the Narcissus flower bloomed. Echo stayed with that flower until she died as well. Her curse, however, did not follow her to the Underworld, but remained on earth.

Odysseus

One of the craftiest heroes in all mythology, Odysseus was a notable character in Homer's Iliad, but his true notoriety became legendary in the poet's sequel, the Odyssey.

Odysseus had done his best to stay out of the Trojan War and remain at home in Ithaca, but it was not to be. He was forced to leave his wife Penelope and his son Telemachus and, sadly, he did not see either one of them for twenty years. For ten years, Odysseus fought for Greece in the Trojan War. It was he who had suggested the strategy of the wooden horse, thus turning the tide against the Trojans.

Odysseus had the Greeks sail away from the walled city of Troy, leaving behind the giant wooden horse and one Greek soldier, Sinon. Sinon told the Trojans that the horse was an acknowledgement of the Trojans' superiority. Most of the Trojans believed Sinon and maneuvered the horse inside the walled city. The horse was filled with several Greek soldiers. During the night, when the Trojans were sleeping off many hours of celebrations, the hidden Greek warriors emerged from the horse and opened the gates of Troy, giving access to the entire Greek army which had been out of sight on board ships located behind an island.

Though the war had ended, Odysseus's trial would continue for another decade. The Greeks had reveled too much in their victory over Troy and did not give proper thanks to the gods. Athena and Poseidon turned against them and sent tempests to vex their ships as they left the obliterated Troy. Odysseus's ship survived, but he had been so far blown off course that he had entered hostile waters filled with islands of enemies. It was not until Athena softened to his plight that Odysseus was able to return to Ithaca.

Oedipus

When King Laius and Queen Jocasta of Thebes had a baby boy, the oracle at Delphi warned them that the child was fated to kill his father and marry his mother. Horrified, but unwilling to kill the child, the King ordered his son to be taken into the faraway mountains. The baby was found by a kindly couple that raised him as their own. When the boy named Oedipus was old enough to understand the ways of the world, he journeyed to Delphi and was given the same prediction. Believing that the parents referred to in the prediction were the ones who had raised him, he immediately left home for Thebes.

During his escape, Oedipus came into conflict with a chariot of royal bullies. A fight ensued and, in the struggle, Oedipus killed King Laius, never realizing that the first part of the oracle's prediction had just come true.

When he reached Thebes, Oedipus learned that the city had come under attack from the Sphinx, one of Echidna's monstrous children. The

Sphinx had the body of a lion, the wings of an eagle, and the head of a woman. The creature delighted in asking a riddle. If the person she asked did not get the answer right, the Sphinx would devour the loser. Oedipus confronted the Sphinx and took up her challenge. She asked, "What has four legs in the morning, two legs in the afternoon, and three legs in the evening?" Oedipus recognized the veiled references to the three stages of life – infancy, maturity, and old age. With the riddle solved, the Sphinx died. Thebes was so thankful to be rid of the scourge of the Sphinx that the citizens offered their widowed Queen Jocasta to him. Oedipus married her, became King, and the prediction was complete.

Eventually, a pestilence came over Thebes, and seers were brought to the city to discern what was happening. The awful truth was soon discovered – nature was revolting over Oedipus's terrible, unwitting sins. Upon hearing the news, Jocasta killed herself and Oedipus put out his own eyes. He roamed the land in exile, his daughter Antigone his only companion. No one would take him in for fear of bringing Oedipus's unspeakable troubles upon their heads. It was the great Athenian Theseus who finally offered Oedipus a safe place to die.

Orpheus

The son of the chief Muse Calliope, Orpheus was the greatest mortal musician who ever lived. So sweetly powerful were his songs that he was capable of making any listener feel whatever emotion his lyre attempted to express. His songs would move even inanimate objects such as rocks and rivers. That sort of power made Orpheus an invaluable member of the Argonauts against the sirens.

After his adventuring, Orpheus married his dearest love, Eurydice, but on the day of the wedding, a serpent bit the girl and she died.

Orpheus sang songs of such desperate sadness that the entire world was overcome by grief. He sang by the entrance of the Underworld hoping his music might move the land of the dead – and it did. For the only time in

his life, Hades wept. Cerberus became tame. The Furies stopped torment-
ing evildoers. The Underworld felt Orpheus's pain.

Hades beckoned Orpheus and told the musician that he could have his
Eurydice back if he left the Underworld with her trailing behind and
without ever looking back at her. Orpheus agreed and made his way back
to the surface with Eurydice walking behind him. Before making it out of
the Underworld, Orpheus's eagerness got the better of him and he turned
around. He saw Eurydice, but only for a moment. Within seconds, she
faded away, returning to the land of the dead.

Orpheus's lamentations became unbearable. His music, now performed
in the lonely forest, saddened the very earth itself. As his despondent verse
traveled through the air, it ruined the revelry of a group of intoxicated
Maenads. The crazed women attacked Orpheus and tore him to pieces, as
was the way of their cult, and tossed his remains into the sea.

Pygmalion

As the King of Cyprus, it was expected of Pygmalion to take a wife and
have children, but he refused. He saw nothing noble in the opposite sex
and spent most of his time in civil or artistic pursuits. One day, he
sculpted the figure of a woman out of ivory and he fell in love with it. The
sculpture was the ideal woman to him. He adorned it in finery and jewels
and spent much time with it.

On the festival of Aphrodite, King Pygmalion prayed most reverently
that his statue – his wife – come to life. The goddess of love granted the
good King's desire and gave life to the statue. The two were very happy
together and had a son named Paphos.

Some sources name the statue Galatea.

Pyramus and Thisbe

Pyramus and Thisbe were two young people who had fallen deeply in
love over the course of their youth. Their parents had homes adjacent to

one another and separated by a wall. Though their families had banned them from ever being together, the two would sneak out late at night and speak words of love through a small hole in the wall.

When the couple could no longer stand to be apart, they planned to meet in the woods. Thisbe arrived at their meeting place first and stumbled upon a lion fresh from the kill. She fled, dropping her cloak in the process. When Pyramus arrived, he saw the lion with dried blood covering its jaws and Thisbe's cloak in its mouth. Assuming that his beloved had been devoured, Pyramus killed himself with his sword.

Thisbe eventually returned, hoping to find Pyramus. She did. So deep was her grief that she took the very weapon that Pyramus had used and she thrust it into her heart.

Scylla and Charybdis

This monstrous duo was the proverbial "rock and a hard place" for sailors.

Scylla's station as a fatal threat to sailors began with Glaucus, a fisherman who had eaten of a special grass. After ingesting the greenery, Glaucus had an overwhelming urge to jump into the sea. He became a sea god.

When Glaucus saw the nymph Scylla bathing near his ocean, he approached her with words of love. Unfortunately, his half man, half fish form frightened her, and she fled. Desperate, Glaucus enlisted the aid of the sorceress Circe to help him woo Scylla.

Circe, though, fell in love with him and refused to help. Glaucus did not return Circe's love, but he managed to awaken her wrath. The sorceress appeared at Scylla's bathing spot while the nymph was wading up to her waist in the ocean water. She poured a terrible potion into the sea. The black magic transformed Scylla's lower body into six ever-snarling giant dog heads. The poor nymph remained attached to the rocks of the straits of Messina, her lower half attacking every ship that passed.

Directly across from Scylla was Charybdis, a monstrous whirlpool. Everyday, the monster swallowed great gulps of ocean and the ships upon it then spat the water back out.

Jason and Odysseus were two of the very few sailors to ever survive a trip between these most fearsome of sea monsters.

BIBLIOGRAPHY

Bulfinch, Thomas. Age of Fable. New York: Harper, 1966.

Christ, Henry I. Myths and Folklore. New York: Amsco School Publications, 1989.

D'Aulaire, Edgar Parin, and Ingri D'Aulaire. Book of Greek Myths. New York: Doubleday, 1962.

Euripides. Medea. Translated by Rex Warner. New York: Dover Publications, 1993.

Hamilton, Edith. Mythology. New York: Mentor, 1969.

Hendricks, Rhoda A. Classical Gods and Heroes. New York: Morrow Quill, 1972.

Herzberg, Max J. Myths and their Meaning. Boston: Allyn and Bacon, 1984.

Hesiod. Theogeny. Translated with an Introduction and Notes by M. L. West. Oxford: Oxford University Press, 1988.

Homer. Iliad. Translated and with an Introduction by Richard Lattimore. Chicago: University of Chicago Press, 1951.

Lévi-Strauss, Claude. Structural Anthropology. New York: Basic Books, 1963.

Murray, Alexander S. Who's Who in Mythology. London: Bracken Books, 1994.

Ovid. Metamorphoses. Translated with an Introduction by Mary M. Innes. London: Penguin, 1955.

Pindar. The Odes. Translated with an Introduction by C. M. Bowra. London: Penguin, 1969.

Vergil. Aeneid. Translated by Charles J. Billson. New York: Dover Publications, 1995.

INDEX